HAND BOOKBINDING
A Manual of Instruction

Aldren A. Watson
Illustrations by the Author

DOVER PUBLICATIONS, INC.
New York

Bibliographical Note

This Dover edition, first published in 1996, is an unaltered, unabridged republication of the work originally published by Macmillan Publishing Company, New York, in 1986.

Library of Congress Cataloging-in-Publication Data

Watson, Aldren Auld, 1917–
    Hand bookbinding, a manual of instruction / by Aldren A. Watson ; illustrations by the author.
        p.   cm.
    Includes index.
    ISBN 0-486-29157-X (pbk.)
    1. Bookbinding—Handbooks, manuals, etc. 2. Handicraft—Handbooks, manuals, etc. I. Title.
Z271.W36 1996
686.3′02—dc20
                                          95-52594
                                            CIP

Manufactured in the United States of America
Dover Publications, Inc., 31 East 2nd Street, Mineola, N.Y. 11501

For Eva Mansfield Auld

and Cammie *and* Thomas

Contents

1

Introduction

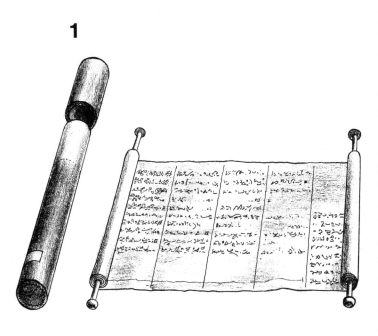

1

2

Paradoxically, the history of bookbinding begins many hundreds of years after the appearance of the first book, one of the earliest examples of which is an Egyptian papyrus roll composed of eighteen columns of hieratic writing, dating from the twenty-fifth century B.C. and stored in a tube "binding" (**1**). The roll form (from the Latin *volumen,* "roll of writing") continued well into the Christian era, when parchment gradually replaced papyrus as a writing material. The arrangement of the writing in parallel columns separated by vertical lines held the potential for the development of an entirely new form. Eventually the idea of cutting the roll into a number of flat panels, each holding three or four columns, inspired a binding that was more convenient to use and that would prove to be more durable.

The first bound book was made up of single sheets hinged along one edge by means of lacing or sewing. In the Latin codex or manuscript book, the columnar arrangement was continued, with typical examples from Roman times having three or four columns to the page. Down to the present day, two- and three-column pages have been in common use, particularly in reference books and textbooks in which short lines contribute to easier reading. Partly for the sake of legibility, modern trade books are predominantly single column and consequently of a smaller trim size than books of earlier times.

Early bindings exhibit all the basic construction elements that characterize modern bindings. They were made up of folded sheets collected into gatherings, or signatures, and sewn onto cords running across their backs. The pages of these books were large, probably much influenced by the size of the animal skins from which the parchment was made (**2**). Subsequently, wooden boards were placed on either side of the sewn signatures—but not attached to them—in positions corresponding to the front and back covers, to protect the book's pages. At some later time it was discovered that the cords to which the signatures were sewn could as easily be laced directly into the edges of the boards to form a more compact and durable unit (**3**). The fundamental evolution of bookbinding was completed when the whole volume was covered with a sheet of leather to conceal the cords and sewing, to reinforce the hinges, and to provide protection and permanence (**4**).

The development of bookbinding is both simple and complex. In the past eighteen hundred years the basic construction of the book has not changed, as an examination of a contemporary binding will show. It is still a series of signatures sewn one to the other at the folds and secured between two boards whose outer surfaces are covered. Just as the perfection of any technique cannot proceed in isolation from other factors, bookbinding has been influenced by many events having nothing directly to do with books or even literature.

The early monastic orders were the guardians of nearly all knowledge in the Middle Ages, with respect to both writing and scholarship. Thus it is not surprising that the same persons to whom these skills were entrusted also assumed the role of bookbinders. Their craftsmanship reflected a thoroughness of education available to only a privileged minority. Hence the beginnings of bookbinding are associated with the church, with ecclesiastical history and literature, and with manuscript reference books.

The large size of early manuscript writing (**5**) was governed by the writing tool itself and

3

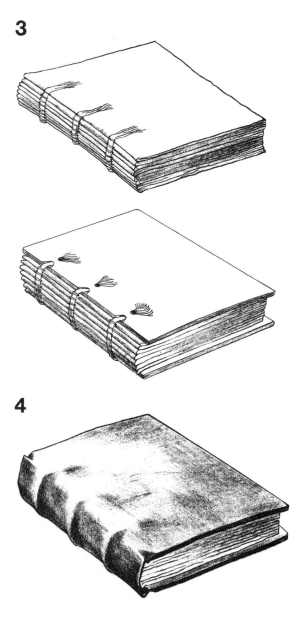

4

demanded a generous page size, while the considerable thickness of the handmade paper was mostly what contributed to the bulk of the bound book. Letter by letter, each word, line, and page was patiently handwritten and usually enhanced with flourished initials illuminated in brilliant colors. The bindings were of leather, their large boards inviting decoration. There are countless examples with richly tooled designs combined with settings of gems, rare stones, and heavy gold leaf (**6**). As a further embellishment, engraved gold clasps or latches were attached to the boards to hold them closed. Working with good materials and virtually unlimited time, the monastery binders produced work of uncompromising quality and durability. These ceremonial reference books were quite literally—then as now—original works of art, intended for the use of only a select few people. Quite apart from their content and visual beauty, perhaps their greatest value lay in the impossibility of replacing them, for many of these limited editions would

5

Dicebant ergo

Et milites

reed pen

6

have been copied from equally unique volumes borrowed with difficulty from another library at a great distance. Needing to be carefully guarded, in the monastery library these rare books were hitched by chains to the shelves or reading tables.

Bookbinding was also affected by the art of papermaking, which was introduced to Europe from China in the tenth century. Sheets of this new handmade material approximated the weight of parchment, but they could be folded, pierced, and sewn with greater ease. As the knowledge of papermaking spread, it was found that the large sheets of this new material need not always be used as a single fold, or folio size (**7**). Paper was pliable enough to withstand being folded several times without damage. Two folds produced the 9 × 12-inch quarto page, and three made a 6 × 9-inch octavo comprising eight leaves, or sixteen pages—a size corresponding closely to the average trim size of a modern book. This readily available material, coupled with an awakened interest in more books on a broadening range of subjects, set the stage for a new phase in the development of bookbinding—the advent of the block book, in which both the text and the illustrations for each page were cut in relief on blocks of wood, one block for each page. Scores of identical impressions could be printed from the blocks, and the blocks could be safely stored and reprinted as required. Although infinitely faster than making duplicate copies one at a time with a reed pen, the task of cutting thousands of individual letters in wood was still enormously tedious.

A development amounting to a revolution came in the fifteenth century with the perfection by Johann Gutenberg of printing from movable type. By this process of composing words from individual type letters, an entire page could be set and hundreds of impressions printed in a relatively short time. Moreover, once the edition of a page had been printed, the type could be sorted, or distributed, and used again to set another page.

7

folio

quarto

octavo

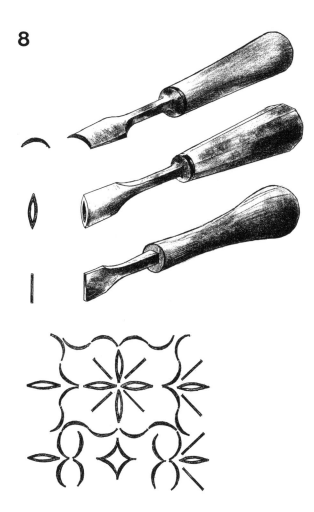

Yet this astonishing invention did not immediately bring about a reduction in the trim size of books, for the early movable type letters were almost exact copies of the handwritten characters of the manuscript and block books. Printing from movable type did, however, dramatically multiply the numbers of books in circulation as well as increase the demand for bookbinders, and it transformed bookbinding from a strictly cottage trade to one of mass production. In the course of time bookbinding moved away from the monasteries into the printers' shops, and ultimately to quite separate binding establishments.

Leather persisted as the covering material, while the recently imported art of blind and gold tooling long practiced in the East gave bookbinding a fresh impetus. The cords on which the signatures were sewn, and which were covered with leather, made pleasing raised bands and set off panels on the backbone of the book. This was to become an important design feature, as the panels were filled with hand-tooled decoration built up with impressions from various small tools (**8**).

European royal families and others of the aristocracy inadvertently sponsored the further development of distinctive binding styles through their patronage of many skilled binders. Coats of arms, crests, and heraldic devices were made the central motifs of bindings that they commissioned for their private libraries. Curiously, these binding styles are known not by the names of the binders but by those who ordered the work. The Grolier bindings, for example, were named for Jean Grolier, Vicomte d'Aguisy, treasurer of France in 1545.

The Industrial Revolution also left its mark on the bookbinding trade. In the early 1900s, concurrent with the machine invasion of every conceivable manufacturing field, binding methods suffered severe and often degrading innovations. Where formerly the tooling of leather had been strictly a hand operation, whole panels of tooling were now machine stamped in a single, swift motion. While this might have been meant to put fine binding within the reach of everyone of modest means, the new stampings lacked the taste and artistry of handwork. Rather than evolving a new decorative style stemming from the machine's possibilities or limitations, this new technique aimed at low cost gave only the superficial impression of handwork while failing to achieve its quality. This revision of standards for the sake of economics was also reflected in the use of cheaper paper, machine-woven cloth, and shortcut binding methods. When cloth tape replaced cords in the sewing operation, an attempt was made to retain the elegant look of hand binding by attaching false bands to the backbone, in imitation of the true, full leather binding (**9**).

The hollow back signaled another new departure—the invention of the *case binding,* in which the cover boards and backbone were glued flat to a sheet of cloth or paper quite independent of the sewn signatures. All titling and decoration was stamped on the flat case, the finished case and signatures then being

9

hollow back with false bands

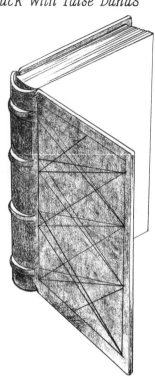

10

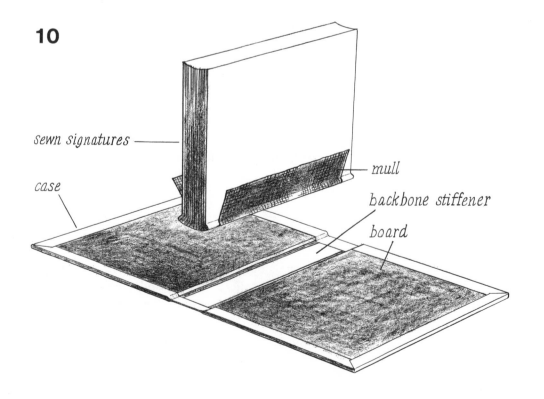

sewn signatures

case

mull

backbone stiffener

board

united and glued to one another by means of a strip of cloth mull and the endsheets (**10**).

By the late 1800s the book had become a permanent democratic property. Machine methods were firmly entrenched and were producing books in almost unlimited quantities at popular prices. It was now that a group of designers and printers, under the leadership of William Morris in England, and an impressive list of craftsmen, typified by T. J. Cobden-Sanderson, were engaged in a revival of sound practices through work done in the many private presses. Concerned with traditional quality bookmaking, these presses used well-designed typefaces, hand typesetting, hand-made paper, hand presses, and good binding methods to produce fine books.

This movement seemed to point out that whereas all bookbinding had once been of remarkably high quality, fine binding had now become a specialized craft, isolated from the book manufacturing industry as a whole and with a very small market consisting of collectors, special libraries, and a limited number of people who appreciated not only a book's content but also the workmanship of its printing and binding.

This book is intended as a manual of instruction in the traditional methods of hand binding and as a reference for students and professionals in publishing and its allied trades.

For further study of bookbinding in general and traditional leather binding in particular, there are numerous excellent books to consult, among them Douglas Cockerell, *Bookbinding and the Care of Books*, London, 1953; Bernard C. Middleton, *The Restoration of Leather Bindings*, Chicago, 1972; and Jeff Clements, *Bookbinding*, London, 1963.

Aldren A. Watson

North Hartland, Vermont

2

Materials, Tools, and Equipment

Materials

The raw materials of bookbinding include paper, woven tape, thread, boards, paste, and fabric, all of which are available in varying grades and qualities. Since the greatest investment in good binding is time, only the best materials should be used. Many of them are rather expensive, yet the additional cost is negligible considering how little goes into any one binding. Sources for materials, tools, and equipment are listed at the end of this chapter.

Paper

Rag content paper is more flexible, more durable, and less likely to yellow than is wood pulp paper. A good quality 16- or 20-pound white wove bond, ledger, or typewriter paper is excellent for making a blank book. There are also available many domestic and imported papers in white, ivory, cream, gray, and other shades that are attractive in themselves or that can be fairly closely matched as endsheets for a book that is to be rebound or repaired. Many of these same rag papers are suitable for covering and lining cover boards, slipcases, and boxes. Covering paper should be strong but of medium weight for ease in pasting and folding. It should also be flexible, to withstand opening and closing of the cover joints, and should have good wearing qualities. When selecting papers, it is wise to make trial folds and turnovers, using scraps, as some papers crackle and break when they are sharply creased.

Tape

Woven twill tape is manufactured of cotton, linen, and polyester. Cotton is more pliable than linen and somewhat easier to paste and manipulate. Polyester has too little body and is therefore not recommended. Of the three types, linen is the heaviest, strongest, and most durable, but because it is filled with a sizing, it usually has to be pasted twice to make it pliable enough to stick down well. Three widths are adequate for almost any work—¼ inch, ⅜ inch, and ½ inch.

Thread

Sewing thread should be strong, soft, and not too fine. Hard finished thread cuts and tears the signature paper when it is drawn up tight and weakens the binding. Linen binder's thread is ideal although it is not always easy to find. A good substitute is a No. 16 or No. 25 mercerized cotton or a No. 18 button and carpet thread. The higher the number, the finer the thread. The common No. 50 used for sewing clothing is too fine for most binding work. Thread should always be waxed before sewing. The wax prevents kinking, holds a knot better, and extends the life of the thread.

Boards

Binding board should be dense and stable, to resist warping when the covering material is pasted down. As paste dries, the material shrinks, pulling one side of the board hollow.

A similar contraction occurs when the endsheet is pasted to the other side of the board. Ideally, the pull of the endsheet equals that of the covering material, and the board returns to its original flat configuration.

The most satisfactory board is known as *binder's board*, a high-quality pulp board made without glue or laminations. In its manufacture, wet pulp webs or blankets are laid one on top of another and hydraulically pressed to remove water, mat the fibers more compactly, and reduce the thickness, or caliper, of the board by approximately one-half. This wet-process pressing provides the essential stability—resistance to distortion—and a density nearly twice that of a wooden board of the same caliper.

Chipboard, which is similar to the backing of drawing paper pads, is an acceptable substitute for small books, but it is not stiff enough for books with a trim size upward of 7 × 9 inches. A more reliable substitute is a good-quality rag content illustration board—not mounting board—that is made in single-ply, two-ply, and three-ply. These boards are much stiffer than even a fairly thick chipboard and have good resistance to warping. For the very large, heavy book, extremely tough cover boards can be made by pasting together the two layers of illustration board and pressing them overnight between blank boards and heavy weights.

Mull

The term *mull* describes a strip of cloth pasted over the tapes and the backs of the signatures after sewing, its function being to unite all the signatures while leaving the backbone of the book flexible. The mull should have a weave open enough to allow good paste penetration, yet enough body to stand up to repeated flexing. White linen fabric is the most durable, with white or unbleached muslin as a good second choice. Keep in mind, though, that unbleached muslin may show through as a shadow when the endsheets are pasted over it, especially if they are of very thin paper.

Paste

Hand bookbinders have long used a paste made of wheat flour and found it entirely satisfactory. It is inexpensive and probably safer than the modern adhesives whose chemical composition may create adverse reactions with the paper and other materials of bookbinding. Boiled wheat paste is simple to prepare and has been known to last for several generations.

To make a thick, smooth paste, measure 1½ cups of cold water into a saucepan. Measure 4 tablespoons of plain white wheat flour into a separate container. Add the flour to the cold water a little at a time, beating it in thoroughly with an eggbeater. Put the saucepan over medium heat and stir the mixture constantly while the water is brought to a boil. Stirring is essential to prevent the mixture burning to the bottom of the pan. When it reaches the boil, remove it from the heat and allow the mixture to cool.

This paste can be thinned to any desired consistency by adding water that has been boiled and cooled. While this paste will mold after several days at room temperature, refrigerating it in a screw-top jar will extend its life to about three weeks. When spots of mold appear, discard the paste and make a fresh batch.

Cloth

Looking at the range of colors, patterns, weaves, and textures in the fabrics available today, it might seem that the choice of cloth for bookbinding is unlimited. Not all fabrics are suitable, however. Aside from its pliability and ease of manipulation, the most important question is how a particular fabric behaves when it is pasted. The only sure way to answer this is to make at least two tests on scraps of each fabric you are considering. In one test apply paste to the wrong side of the cloth and attach it to a small piece of binder's board; and in the other spread paste only on the board. With some fabrics the paste will settle on the wrong side and stay there, and with others it will strike clear through to the good side of the fabric, leaving a highly visible blemish when the paste dries. And depending on the fabric, the paste may react with the dyes and cause the color to bleed or actually to change.

In these respects binder's buckram has some advantage over other fabrics. It is a specially woven cloth impregnated with a sizing that prevents strikethrough of the paste. However, most buckram is rather stiff and springy and requires patience to stick it down well. And the colors are limited in number and generally not as interesting as those available in other fabrics.

Tools and Equipment

Some of the tools listed here may already be on hand, a number of them can be homemade from directions in the section *Making Tools and Equipment* (see pp. 147–157), and others can be obtained from sources listed at the end of this chapter.

Carpenter's square, 16 x 24 inches

An essential tool for accurate cutting of paper and board. There are smaller models on the market, but the weight of this professional steel square gives a decided nonslip advantage for all cutting operations.

Steel ruler, 18 inches

For measuring, light cutting and trimming, and for other straight-edge work such as scoring and folding.

Knives

A utility or mat-cutting knife is an inexpensive rugged tool for all cutting jobs. It has a large, safe handle grip and uses replaceable blades.

An X-Acto knife, also with replaceable blades, is better for light cutting and trimming.

Razor blade

Because of its very thin steel, a single-edge razor blade is superior for cutting paper. It is also fine for cutting boards, but—again because of the thin steel—the blade must be held perpendicular to avoid its being bent under pressure and broken.

Shears

A pair of 8-inch dressmaker's shears with offset handles is particularly good for cutting fabric.

Flat folder

A superior tool for folding and creasing signature paper and cloth, and easily made at home.

Folding stick

Does the work of the conventional bone folder, but I prefer this homemade version because of its large handle.

Folding needle

Another homemade tool, indispensable for fine work where even the most slender finger is too clumsy.

Right-angle card

A miniature square especially useful in close quarters, such as when squaring up the head of a book before attaching the mull. Much more convenient than a carpenter's try square.

Squared card

Especially for checking the overhang, or square, of cover boards, but also useful as a square.

Sewing frame

This is an essential piece of equipment. It holds the tapes taut in the correct position and has a platform on which to lay the signatures being sewn, leaving both hands free for the job of sewing. Commercial sewing frames are made with wooden screw adjustments to tighten the tapes, but they are expensive. An entirely adequate sewing frame can be made at home, although its tape-tightening device is not as convenient.

Press and tub

Perhaps the most indispensable piece of binding equipment. There is no substitute for a press and a tub or stand to hold it, although a very satisfactory press can be built at home for a fraction of the cost of a commercial one. However, if you should contemplate buying a press, a *lying press* is a better investment than a *finishing press*. With sloping jaws on one side for finishing work and a track on the other for a plow or trimming device to slide in, the lying press does the work of both.

Ready-made sewing frames and presses are made of select hardwoods and, if stored in a moderately cool and dry atmosphere, will last almost indefinitely. Excessive heat and humidity warps the wooden parts and is especially destructive of the turned wooden screws used in both these pieces of equipment.

Paste brushes

A ⅞-inch round paste brush is excellent for all general work, and a No. 5 artist's bright oil painting brush (shorter, stiffer bristles) for fine work such as pasting the mitered corners of turnovers. The bristles should be somewhat stiff, not excessively long, and a bit springy. A limp brush will not spread paste.

Piercing awl

One tool that is better homemade. This awl should be slender, with a fine point. Carpenter's scratch awls are much too coarse.

Beeswax

For treating sewing thread. A ¼-pound chunk will last a long time.

Sandpaper

No. 120 grit flint or silicon carbide paper. One sheet cut into four pieces will last for a good many book jobs.

Needles

One package of 1/5 sharps or 3/9 milliner's needles. Both have eyes that can be easily threaded yet are not grossly larger than the shank of the needle.

Wastepaper

The most efficient disposable paper for pasting work is a 14 × 17-inch pad of newsprint.

Rubbing Sheets

Vellum tracing paper has just the right surface for the work of rubbing down pasted materials and the added advantage of being nearly transparent. The 14 × 17-inch pads are the most convenient.

Note: Do not use newspapers for either wastepaper or rubbing sheets. The printing ink transfers to the work and is nearly impossible to clean off.

Workbench

The first requisite is a flat, smooth, and solid work surface. A long wooden table makes a good bench, but two or three smaller ones work just as well. Cover the top with clean brown wrapping paper stretched flat and taped tightly over all four edges. Use one end of the bench for cutting, trimming, and folding; the center for sewing; and the other end for pasting. Tape a sheet of thick cardboard over the cutting section to protect the bench and to ensure sharp, clean edges on cut paper.

Good lighting is important. A 4-foot fluorescent tube or a pair of scissor clamp drop lights will provide plenty of illumination.

Have a large carton under the bench for efficient disposal of paste-soiled wastepaper. Collect and stack a supply of cotton cloths at the back edge of the bench, along with a water jar for removing paste from the work, hands, and tools.

Collect and have at hand a supply of weights for pressing: six or eight large, heavy books such as encyclopedias and half a dozen clean bricks tightly wrapped and taped in clean paper. If possible also reserve a separate table where pasted work can be pressed and left undisturbed to dry.

Sources for Materials, Tools, and Equipment

MAIL ORDER CATALOGS

Cloth, papers, tools, and general bookbinding supplies

Andrews-Nelson-Whitehead
31-10 48 Avenue
Long Island City, NY 11101

Basic Crafts
1201 Broadway
New York, NY 10001

Talas Division of
Technical Library Service Inc.
213 West 35 Street
New York, NY 10001

J. Hewitt & Sons Ltd
97 St. John Street
London EC1M 4AT
England

Russell Bookcrafts
94 Bancroft
Hitchin
Hertsford, England

Gane Brothers & Lane Inc.
Mail Order Catalog Division
1400 Greenleaf Avenue
Elk Grove Village, IL 60007

ART SUPPLY STORES

beeswax
boards: gray chipboard, hot-pressed illustration board
brushes: paste, sable lettering
colors: designer's gouache
eraser: soft vinyl
fixatif: aerosol workable
india ink: jet black waterproof
knives: utility and X-Acto, with extra blades
papers: white bond, bristol board, charcoal drawing, white and colored cover, newsprint, vellum tracing
pen points: lettering and calligraphy
ruler: 18-inch steel
shears
triangle: 90-degree
varnish: clear picture

BUILDING MATERIALS DEALERS

boards: birch, maple, pine, other plywood

FABRIC AND SEWING STORES

beeswax
embroidery twist
fabric: cotton, linen, silk, other
knitting needles
muslin: unbleached and white
needles
shears
thread
twill tape: cotton and linen

HARDWARE STORES

back saw
block plane
cord: headband
dowels
file: double-cut
glue: carpenter's wood
hand drill and points
miter box
paint thinner
pliers
polyurethane
sandpaper
screws: flathead brass and steel
sharpening stone: combination
square: 16×24-inch carpenter's
tack rag

STATIONERY STORES

bond typewriter paper
cord: headband
fiberboard binders
paper punch
writing paper

3

Fundamental Procedures

11

12

13

There are six principal stages in the hand binding of a book (**11–16**). Taken as a group, they make up what at first may seem a very complicated procedure, but the complete process of bookbinding proves much simpler when the numerous steps are considered individually and in sequence.

Preparing the signatures (**11**) Assuming a blank notebook is to be bound, sheets of paper are cut and squared to uniform size. They are then divided into gatherings of equal numbers of sheets and folded to make signatures. As each one is folded, it is signed or marked with a number on the back edge next to the fold, hence the term *signature*. The signatures are then collated by putting these numbered gatherings in the proper sequence.

Sewing up (**12**) To bind all the signatures into a flexible unit, they are sewn to tapes running across the backs of the signatures. Sewing through the folds of the signatures not only holds them securely to the tapes but also creates the flexibility for the pages to turn freely and for the book to open flat.

Attaching the mull (**13**) To consolidate the sewing and reinforce the backbone of the book, a strip of cloth *mull* is glued to the backs of the signatures. The mull and tapes together provide the means of attaching the sewn signatures to the boards.

Attaching the boards (**14**) Boards are now attached to either side of the sewn signatures, to hold them flat and to protect the exposed edges of the book pages. The boards are made slightly larger than the pages to allow a *square,* or overhang, on the three open sides. The book is thus supported on the edges of the cover boards rather than on the edges of the pages.

Covering the boards (**15**) To protect the backs of the signatures and at the same time conceal the sewing, cloth or paper is wrapped clear around the book, attached, and turned in over the edges of the cover boards.

Pasting the endsheets (**16**) As the final step in construction, the endsheets— the first and last pages—are pasted to the insides of the cover boards, covering the tapes and mull as well as the turned-in edges of the covering material, and adding further reinforcement to the hinges. With this stage completed, the book may be said to be bound.

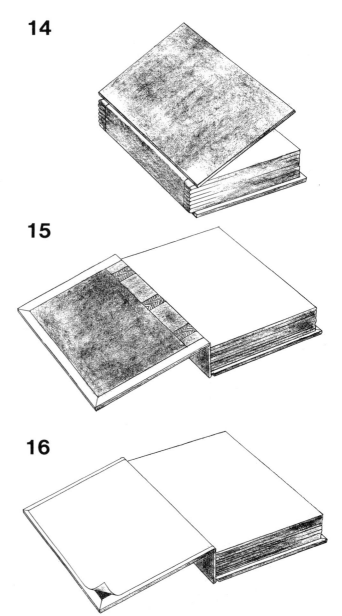

14

15

16

Good workmanship in carrying a binding through these six stages depends to a large extent on practicing and developing a second-nature proficiency with the few basic skills that are demanded repeatedly in the several technical methods used to complete each stage.

Measuring

Accurate measuring is one of the first requirements in binding. Whether the material is paper, board, or cloth, be as precise as possible. The 18-inch steel ruler is graduated in inches and sixteenths, and some in metric measure as well. Other rulers made for the graphic arts also have pica and agate graduations. When a measurement does not fall exactly on the graduations of a particular ruler, use a strip of paper (**17**). Mark the measurement on the strip

17

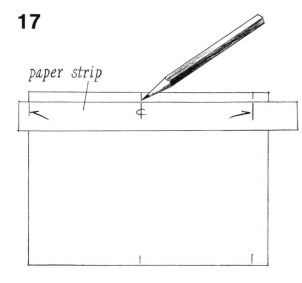

paper strip

18

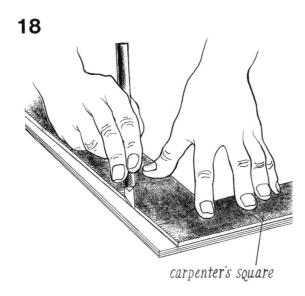

carpenter's square

with a sharp pencil, then transfer it to the work.

While the carpenter's square is also graduated in inches and sixteenths, it is too clumsy for accurate measuring because the thickness of its arms—roughly ⅛ inch—introduces errors as a result of sighting down over its edge to the paper.

Cutting

Paper, board, and cloth should be squared up before cutting to exact size. Handmade and even machine-made papers are rarely perfectly square on the corners. To square the material, lay one arm of the carpenter's square even with one edge (**18**). Hold the square down tight with one hand, and use the other to draw the knife along the edge of the square's other arm. Keep the knife snug against the edge of the square. Then turn the material, align one arm of the square with the freshly cut edge, and make the second cut. Continue in this way, always working from the clean-cut edge, until all four corners are squared.

For the best results, cut only three or four sheets of paper at a time. Attempting to cut ten or a dozen at once will produce wavy, uneven edges that cannot be folded or finished neatly. Use moderate pressure on the knife and make several light cuts rather than one or two heavy ones. Keep firm pressure on the square until the last sheet has been cut. When only one or two sheets are cut, hold the top edge of the waste with a finger to prevent the knife from pulling the paper and tearing out the corner at the end of the stroke (**19**).

Patterned papers should be cut so that the direction of the pattern runs parallel to the edges of the finished work. A paper mask helps to determine the best cutting position (**20**).

When cutting board, hold the square down with plenty of pressure to prevent its slipping, and make numerous light cuts. A clean, square edge can easily be made in this way. When heavy cuts are used, the knife runs off and usually undercuts, producing beveled

19

20

hold the top edge with a finger

square   *waste*

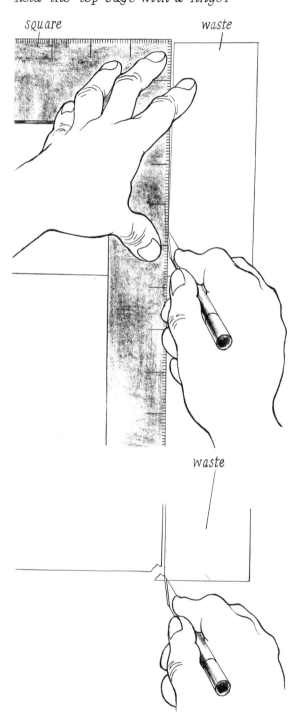

waste

determining cutting position

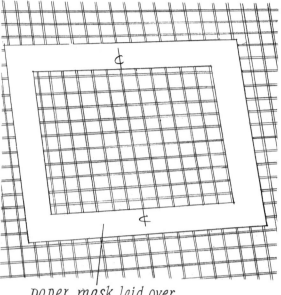

paper mask laid over
patterned cover material

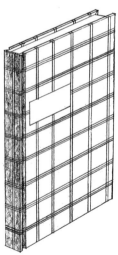

21

wooden block and sandpaper

22

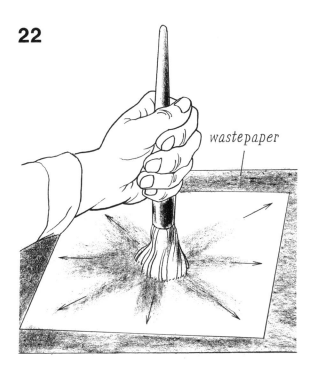

wastepaper

or wobbly edges that cannot be nicely finished. When paper is pasted over such an edge, there will be air pockets and wrinkles.

After cutting the board to size, slightly round the edges with 120-grit sandpaper held over a wooden block (**21**). Paper and cloth adhere better to a rounded edge and wear much longer than when stretched over a sharp edge.

The best tool for cutting fabric is a pair of shears. A sharp knife and the carpenter's square can sometimes be used, but the square must be held down with extreme pressure to keep the cloth from creeping. The weave in some fabrics is uniform enough that cutting along a pulled thread will give accurate results. Patterned fabric should be cut with the same attention to direction as is given to patterned paper (**20**).

Binder's buckram can be cut the same way as paper, although the selvage edges should first be trimmed off.

Pasting

While this may appear a simple enough operation, the difference between an expertly done binding and a second-rate one is often nothing more than carelessly applied paste. The aim is to spread a thin, even coat of paste over the work. Lumps and streaks prevent the pasted paper or cloth from lying flat and smooth, and they trap air bubbles.

Lay the work to be pasted on a clean sheet of wastepaper. Do not use old newspapers or magazines as wastepaper: even if your fingers don't pick up the printing ink, the paste brush certainly will, and the ink will transfer to the brush, the work, and to the paste jar as well.

Hold the work down firmly by an edge. Pick up some paste on the end of the brush. Starting in the center of the work, use a fair amount of pressure to spread paste out toward the edges (**22**). This allows holding the work without the free hand becoming sticky, and it delivers paste to the edges of the work last, ensuring that they will be stuck down securely.

Pasting should be done briskly but not hurriedly. Spread too slowly, the paste begins to dry before the work can be stuck down properly, while if too much speed is attempted, the paper is likely to be buckled or creased. As soon as the paste has been spread, pick up the work with one hand, and with the other discard the soiled wastepaper. Lay the work paste-side down on the material to which it is being attached. Immediately lay a clean rubbing sheet over the work, and with a clean cloth rub down the pasted work, again working from the center toward the edges (**23**). This motion smooths the work flat and forces any air bubbles out to the edges. The rubbing sheet prevents soiling the surface of the work and provides a smooth surface for the cloth to glide over. When the work has been rubbed down, discard the rubbing sheet.

Before starting the actual work, it is productive to do a few trial pasting jobs with scrap paper and board, to establish a clean and tidy pasting routine. Then inspect the results. An isolated paste spot or two can be removed by moistening the corner of a clean cloth with water—the tongue is even better—and gently wiping the spot. But this treatment does not work on all materials. For example, it dulls the surface of buckram and tends to pull up and roughen the fibers of some types of paper.

Pressing

After pasting, attaching, and rubbing down, the work should promptly be pressed under weights to hold it flat until it is completely dry, especially in the case of large areas such as cover boards. Any material, and especially paper, begins to expand when it is pasted. When it is attached to a board the process is reversed, and as the paste dries, the material shrinks back to its original size, pulling one side of the board with it and at the same time producing some warp.

When paper or some other material is pasted to the other side of the board, however,

23

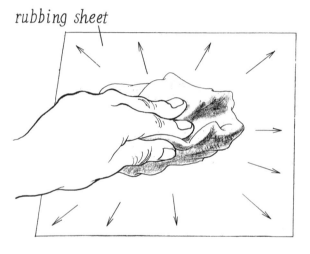

rubbing sheet

24

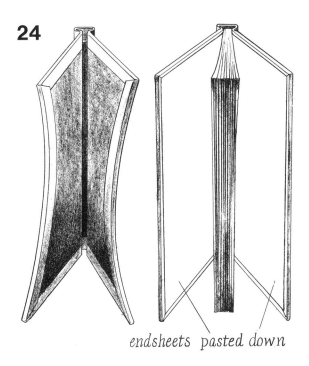

endsheets pasted down

an equal pull is exerted to bring the board back to its normal flat condition (**24**). Of course, this theory does not hold up when a heavy cloth is attached to one side of a board and only a thin paper endsheet is pasted to the other. In general, the heavier the material, the more pull it will exert. Some thought must therefore be given to this effect when selecting materials.

To press pasted work, lay it on a clean sheet of waxed paper spread flat on the bench. Lay another sheet of waxed paper over the work, and on top lay a blank board or a piece of ⅛-inch-thick hard cardboard to distribute the pressure. Then arrange weights on top of the board, making sure they are centered over the work underneath. When using books and bricks for weights, lay the bricks down first and stack books on top to keep the center of gravity low. Use enough books or bricks—or both—to produce at least twenty to thirty pounds of weight. The more weight the better.

In the case of a finished binding, lay pieces of board over both covers just back of the hinges to prevent crushing them (**25**). Let the work stand overnight to dry.

25

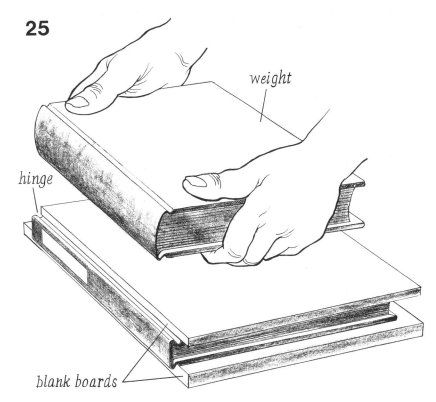

weight

hinge

blank boards

26

27

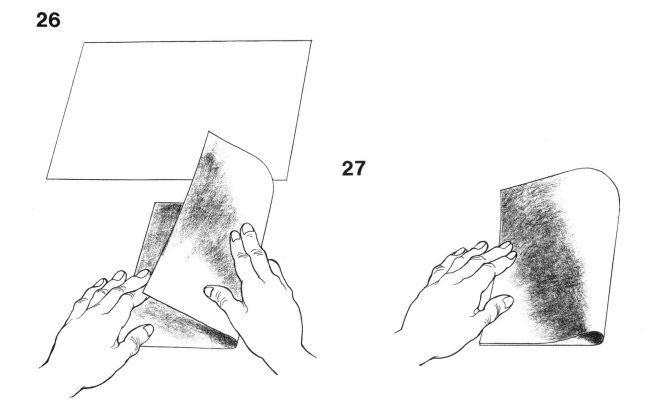

4

Technical Methods

These detailed procedures are common to nearly all bookbinding, even though particular projects may require modifications or changes in the order in which they are carried out.

Folding

Folding is the foundation on which a good binding is built, for it is the sewing through the folds of the signatures that creates both the strength and the flexibility.

For the best visibility while aligning the edges of the pages, work with the top edge of the paper toward you. Fold from one side to the other. One hand guides the corners of the sheet into alignment and holds them there, while the other starts the fold. Use the flat folder to finish this kind of fold. It does a better job than the fingers and keeps the work clean.

Single fold   Make a few trial single folds using ordinary white bond typewriter or mimeograph paper. Lay a sheet of paper on the bench with its top edge toward you. While holding down one half of the sheet, pick up the other half and roll it over to bring the corners into alignment (**26**). Hold them there with one hand (**27**). With the thumb of the other, press down to make a short crease (**28**). Hold the top edges in alignment. Then use the flat folder

28

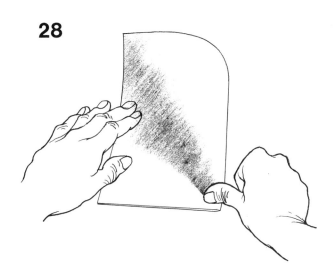

29

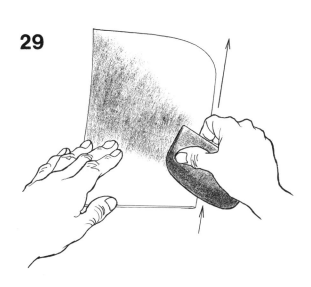

held at a low angle to run a crease away from you the full length of the sheet (**29**). Use only moderate pressure on the folder; too much will cockle the paper.

Folding a signature   A signature consists of several sheets folded as one unit, the exact number depending on the weight, or thickness, of the paper. The fold must have enough substance for the sewing to hold securely without the thread cutting into or tearing the paper, yet not so much bulk that the rounded backs of the signatures are grossly oversize (**30**). While it might be easier to fold the sheets separately and then assemble them one inside the other, the several sharp creases cause the signature—and ultimately the book—to spring open (**31**). And this method as well gives the backs of the signatures a surface composed of sharp edges to which it is impossible to attach the mull without the paste leaking through between signatures.

To make a trial signature, gather four sheets of white bond paper and jog them by tapping their top edges and then the side edges on the bench to align them (**32**). Without disturbing the alignment, lay the sheets on the bench with their top edges toward you. Hold the left half of the sheets firmly with one hand to prevent them from slipping while you pick up the right half and roll the sheets over to the left. The motion is the same as when folding a

30

too few signatures,
too much paper in each

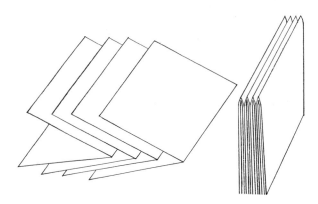

more signatures of less bulk
make a stronger, more durable binding

31

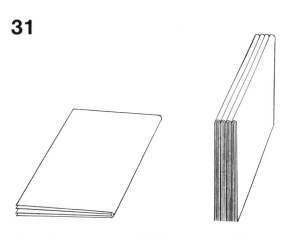

signature sheets folded as one unit   *sheets folded separately*

single sheet, but it takes a little practice to guide the several corners into alignment. The fore edges of the sheets will form a slight V (**33**). Hold the sheets in alignment with one hand and start the crease with the thumb of the other. Then use the flat folder to run the crease away from you. Use moderate pressure to avoid cockling the paper.

32

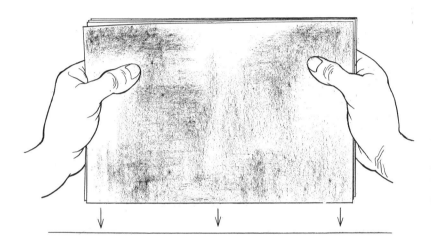

33

fore edge

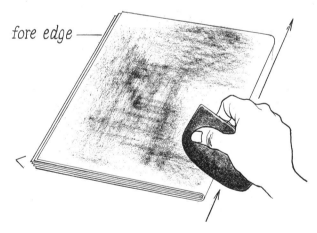

34

French fold

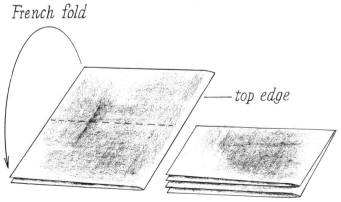

top edge

French fold This is a two-stage fold often used to add bulk or elegance to the binding of single items such as poems or other brief works (**34**). Single-fold a sheet of white bond paper as described. Then turn the work so that the folded side is toward you. Pick up the doubled sheet by the right corner and roll it over to meet the left corner. Align the top edges (which are now folds). Note that a box may form at the second fold, due to the double thickness of paper (**35**). In this case slip the end of the folding stick flat into the box and use some tension on the edge of the stick to pull the box out to a neat edge (**36**). Then make the usual starting crease with a thumb and finish it with the flat folder.

35

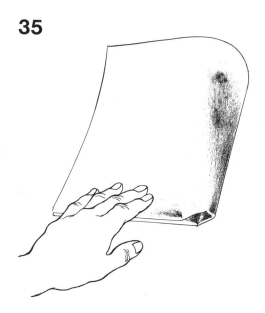

36

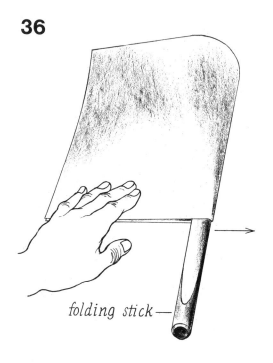

folding stick—

Before folding signatures for a finished binding, make several trial signatures using cheap material such as newsprint or mimeograph paper. Practice single folds, signatures, and French folds until you can manipulate the paper readily and with a degree of accuracy.

Collating

This means to examine and verify that the various parts of a book are complete and in the proper sequence before being sewn up. Collating is especially important in rebinding books, particularly if there are inserts, maps, new material, or new endsheets. But it is also useful in making a blank book, simply as a way to establish the habit of marking, or signing, each signature with a number to ensure that everything is in the correct order (**37**).

37

38

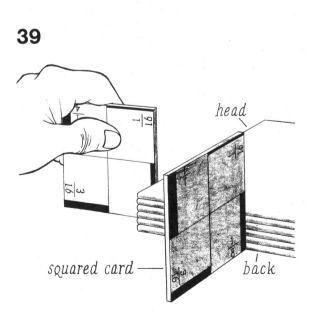

head

Marking up for sewing

In the next stage pencil marks are drawn across the backs of the signatures to position the tapes and to provide a guide for piercing holes for the sewing.

Gather up all the signatures and jog them lightly to align the heads and backs of the signatures (**38**). Lay the signatures on the bench and even up the head and the back, using the squared card (**39**), then lay a weight on them to prevent them from slipping.

Next determine how many tapes of what width are needed. A small, slim book with only a few signatures may need only a pair of ¼-inch tapes. A book the size and bulk of an average novel might require two ⅜-inch tapes, while a very large book of considerable bulk should probably have four ½-inch tapes (**40**). Because the tapes must support the weight of the sewn signatures as well as hold them se-

40

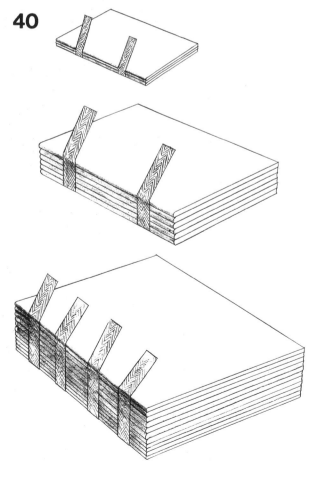

39

squared card —

head

back

curely to the boards, it is preferable to use wider tapes and more of them rather than risk weakening the binding by making the construction only just adequate.

Assuming that three tapes will be used, draw eight marks across the backs of the signatures, using the squared card: one mark ½ inch from the head for the kettlestitch, a similar mark at the foot for the other kettlestitch, and two marks for each tape spaced evenly between (**41**). The tape marks should be spaced a fraction wider than the exact width of the tape;

41

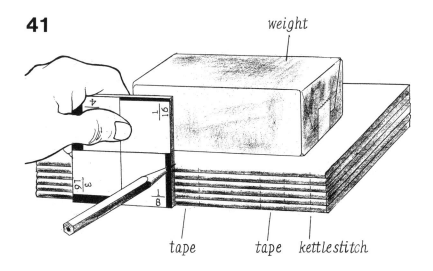

weight

tape　　*tape*　*kettlestitch*

otherwise it will be puckered when the sewing is drawn tight (**42**). The kettlestitches carry the sewing thread from one signature to the next at the head and foot, tying them all together in a series of chainlike knots.

42

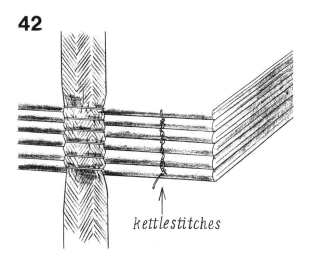

kettlestitches

43

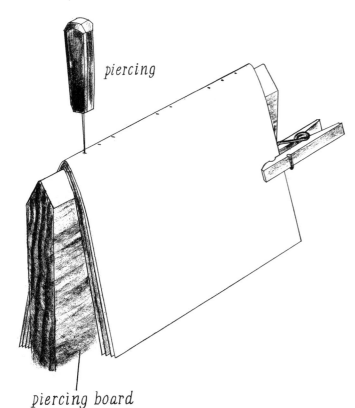

piercing

piercing board

Piercing

All the holes for sewing are pierced in advance to make sure they will be accurately placed in the center of the signature folds. Put the piercing board in the press. Open the first signature to the center and clip a clothespin over one edge to keep the sheets from slipping. Drop the signature over the piercing board. With a thin piercing awl, pierce a hole at each pencil mark, piercing from the outside to the center of the signature (**43**). Push the awl through just far enough so that the hole can easily be located on the inside with the point of the needle. The pierced holes should be smaller in diameter than the sewing thread so that the paper will grip the thread when it is drawn through (**44**).

44

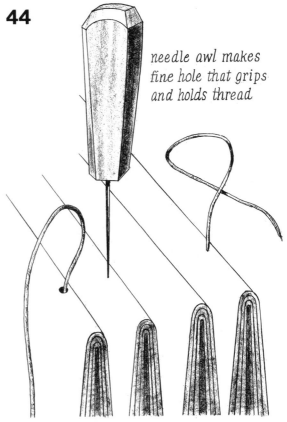

needle awl makes fine hole that grips and holds thread

sewing goes slack in hole pierced with conventional scratch awl

Setting up the frame

Cut three tapes about 14 inches long and attach them to keys as shown in the illustration (**45**). Then feed the tapes up through the slot in the sewing frame, and attach their other ends to the crossbar (**46**). This length of tape allows for ample working space between the crossbar and the platform. Short tapes bring the crossbar too low and interfere with good visibility. Tighten the crossbar to take up the slack in the tapes (**47**).

45

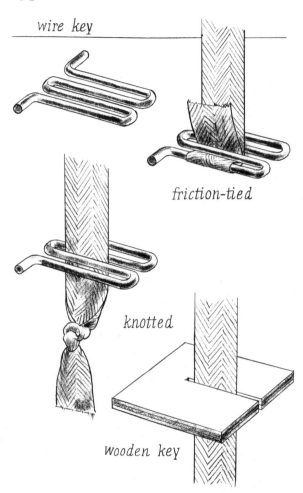

wire key

friction-tied

knotted

wooden key

46

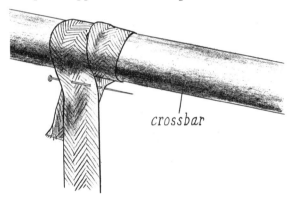

tape wrapped twice and pinned

crossbar

47

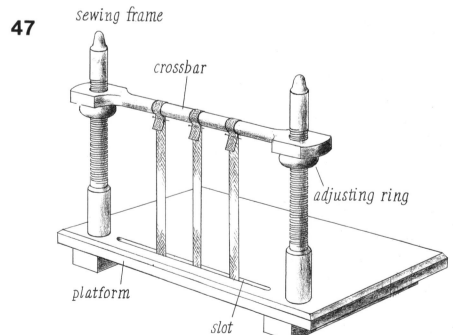

sewing frame

crossbar

adjusting ring

platform

slot

Lay one of the signatures on the platform and shift the tapes right or left until they align with the pencil marks on the signature. Then use a square if necessary to adjust the tapes on the crossbar so they are at right angles to the platform. Tighten the crossbar to make the tapes taut.

Sewing up

Thread a needle with a 30-inch length of thread—about the maximum length for convenient sewing. Wax the thread by pinching it against the beeswax and drawing it through two or three times clear to the end (**48**). Waxing the thread facilitates sewing, prevents the thread from kinking and extends its life. After waxing, tie a knot in the free end, leaving a 3-inch tail beyond the knot.

Sew up the book from the back to the front. Lay the last signature on the sewing frame platform with the pencil marks lined up with the tapes. Slide one hand inside the center of the signature to hold it open (**49**). With the other hand push the needle in at the foot kettlestitch hole and catch the needle on the inside of the signature (**50**). Draw the thread through and snug up against the knot. Take the needle

48

beeswax

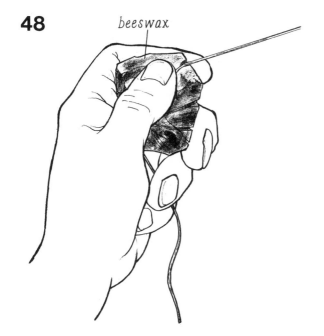

49

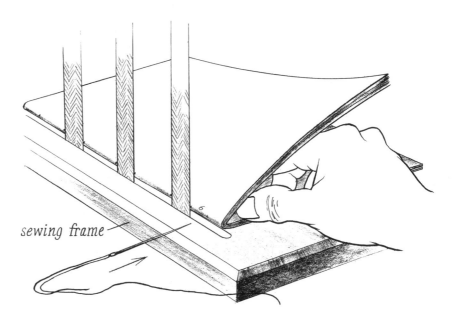

sewing frame

50

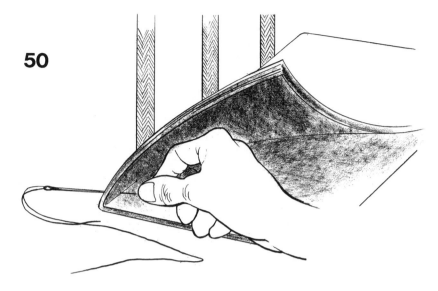

51

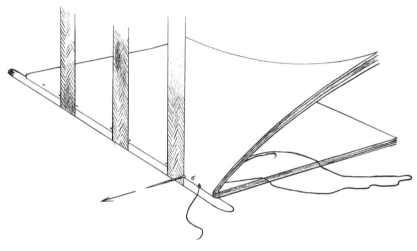

52

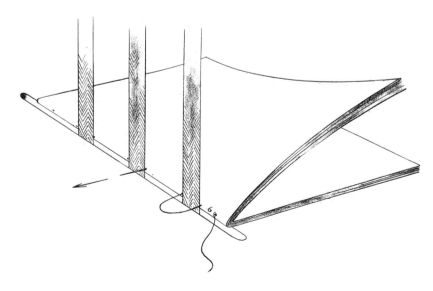

out through the hole below the bottom tape (**51**) and draw the thread snug. Go over the tape and push the needle into the hole above it (**52**). Continue sewing in and out and over the tapes, bringing the needle out through the head kettlestitch hole. Hold the thread out straight, in line with the back of the signature, and draw the thread up snug but not excessively tight (**53**).

Lay the next signature on top of the first and open it to the center. Slide one hand inside. Take the needle in through the head kettlestitch hole, then sew in and out and over the

53

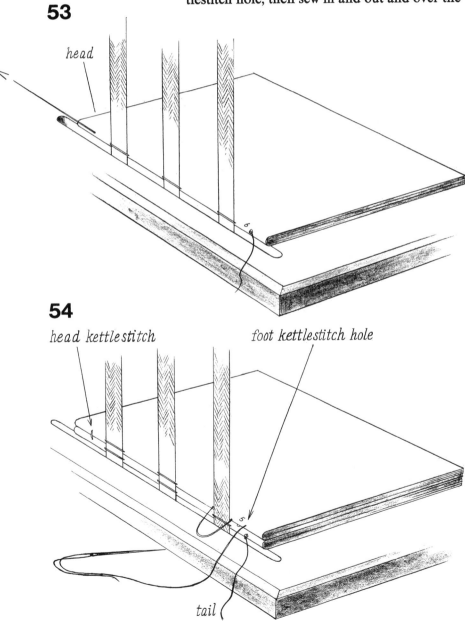

head

54

head kettlestitch   *foot kettlestitch hole*

tail

tapes as before, bringing the needle out at the foot kettlestitch hole (**54**). Draw the thread snug but not so tight that it cuts a gash in the paper (**55**).

Now tie these first two signatures together with a kettlestitch. Pick up the knotted tail of thread in one hand and throw a loop *around and under* the knot. Pass the needle through the loop and draw the thread into a tight stitch (**56**).

Using this basic sewing technique, sew on the remaining signatures in the same way. Note that the next kettlestitch and all subsequent ones are tied as shown in the illustration (**57**). They should be firm and tight while at the same time allowing some flexibility in the binding. If they are drawn up and tied with excessive tension, the back of the book may cave in (**58**) or the signature may be torn, or both.

56

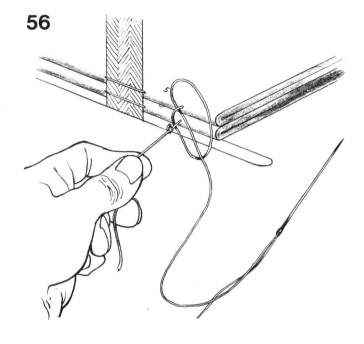

55

57

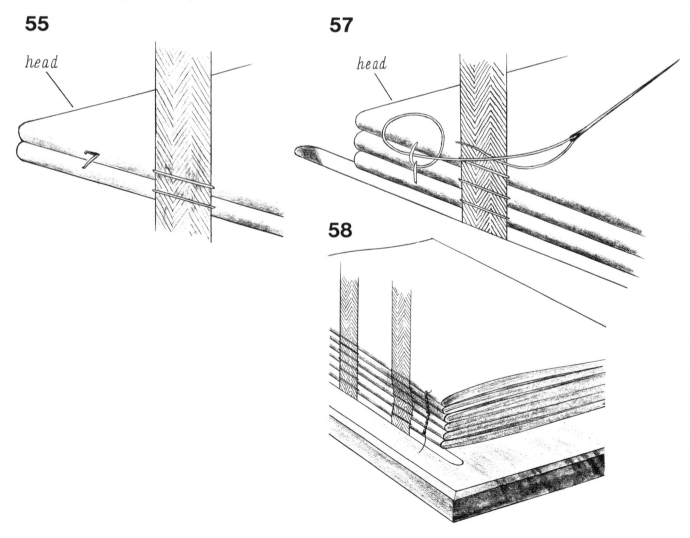

58

Splicing thread

Since to make sewing more convenient the original thread was made only 30 inches long, it will be necessary to splice on a new length when the unused portion has dwindled to 5 or 6 inches. Make the splice as follows: Just after the needle has passed to the outside of a signature, but before going over the tape into the next hole, cut off the thread right next to the eye of the needle (**59**). Tie this loose end to a new 30-inch length of waxed thread by making

59

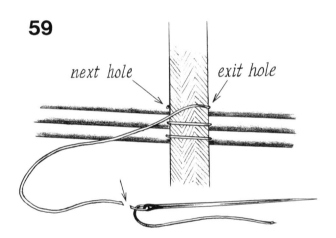

next hole   exit hole

60

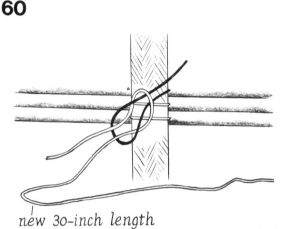

new 30-inch length

a square knot as close as possible to the exit hole (**60**). If the splicing knot is too close to the next hole, it will jam there and cause a weakening slack in the sewing that has been completed to this point. Before pulling the square knot tight, slip the end of the new thread up through the center of the knot, then hold both loose ends together and pull the knot tight to lock it (**61**).

61

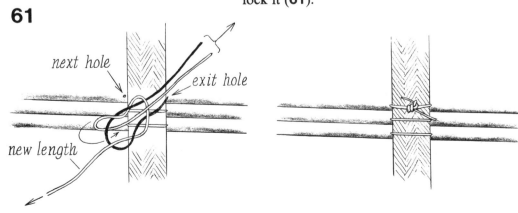

next hole   exit hole

new length

When the last signature has been sewn on, tie off the final kettlestitch with a double knot to lock it. Then trim off the thread, leaving a ¼-inch tail. Cut the tapes loose from the sewing frame, leaving them as long as possible, and pull them taut from both sides to eliminate the puckering (**62**).

62

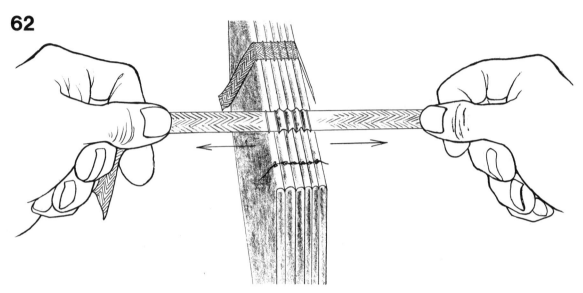

On a very bulky book with many signatures, a swelling develops due to the numerous threads lying inside the signatures. This swelling can be somewhat reduced during sewing by beating down every two or three signatures with a *loaded stick* to force the threads into the paper and further compact the folds of the signatures (**63**). The swelling can be reduced a bit more by tying together the sewing threads over the middle tape (**64**). Slide the needle carefully under the threads and tie each group individually. Groups of three or four threads can be tied, but do not gather too many in a group or draw them too tight, otherwise the back of the book may be caved in or the sewing threads may gash the paper next to the tapes.

63

loaded stick

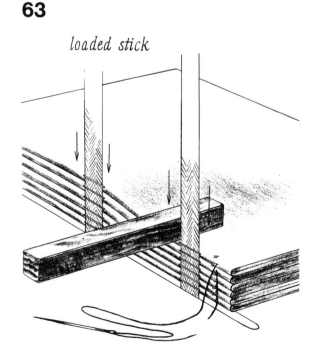

Attaching the mull

At this stage—the sewing having been completed—the book has a tendency to gape open between the first and second signatures and between the last two. To remedy this, these

64

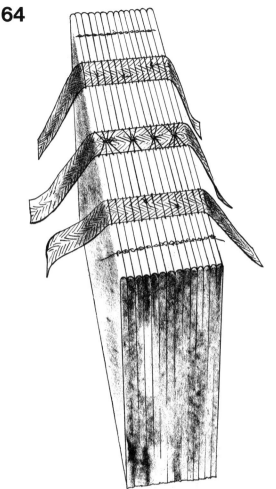

pairs of signatures are lightly pasted together along their back edges (**65**). Lay the sewn signatures faceup on the bench, with the first one opened onto a blank board for support. Lay a clean sheet of wastepaper on top of the second signature 3/32 inch from the back edge. Hold it without slipping while you brush a very thin coat of paste along this narrow exposed edge. Then carefully remove and discard the soiled wastepaper. Close the first signature back in place and press down all along the hinge. Turn the book over and paste together the last two signatures in the same way. Put the work under weights to dry for an hour.

The mull is a cloth strip pasted to the backs of the signatures and to the tapes. It extends either side and is attached with the tapes to the cover boards. Cut a piece of mull long enough to cover the head and foot kettle-stitches, and 3 inches wider than the bulk of the book. Put sheets of waxed paper either side of the sewn signatures and put them in the press with the backbone about ½ inch above the press. Tighten the press just enough to hold the work. Manipulate the signatures into align-

65

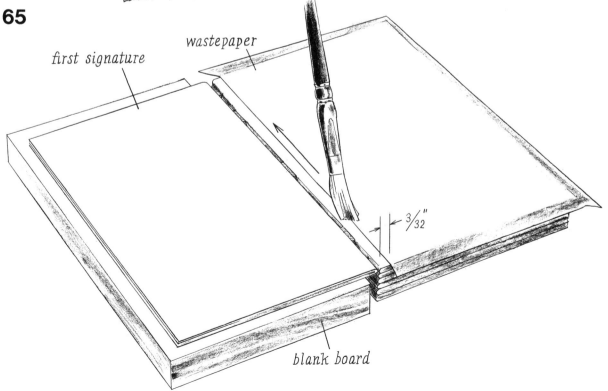

first signature

wastepaper

3/32"

blank board

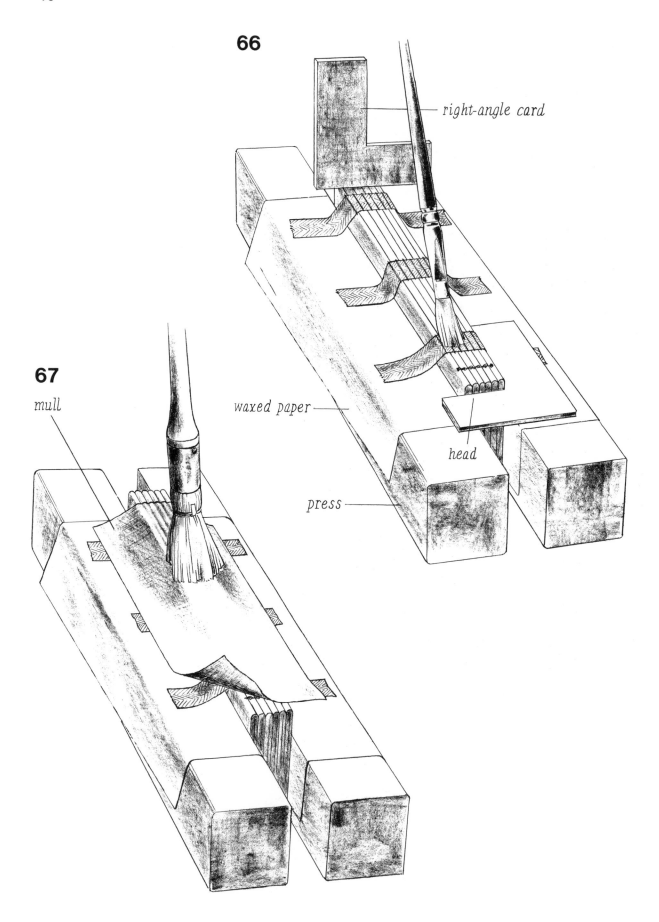

66

right-angle card

waxed paper

head

press

67

mull

ment—square at the head and flat across the back—checking it both ways with the right-angle card (**66**). Tighten the press. Lay the mull on clean wastepaper and brush it with paste, working it well into the weave. Also brush paste onto the backs of the signatures, working some extra paste into the tapes with the fingers. The object is to paste thoroughly without building up so thick a layer that it will crack and weaken the binding. Pick up the pasted mull and lay it on the backbone, centering it in both directions. Give the mull another light brushing of paste (**67**), then use the fingers to work the mull well down on the signatures and over the tapes. Do not paste the free ends of the tapes. Leave the work in the press to dry overnight.

Making boards

There are three boards for the binding illustrated here: front cover, back cover, and backbone strip. Books that are rounded and backed have only the two cover boards, the backbone being stiffened by a strip of heavy paper pasted inside the covering material or fitted with a hollow back.

Although durability requires using a board no thinner than about 1/16 inch, keep in mind that the larger and heavier the book, the heavier the board should be.

Using the carpenter's square and a sharp knife, cut the cover boards, allowing a square of 1/8 inch at the head, fore edge, and foot, and the thickness of two boards at the hinge (**68**). A very large and heavy book may require more square to hold the pages clear of the shelf, but in general a smaller square will withstand more abuse than a large one.

To make the backbone board, first determine its width by measuring the combined thickness of the sewn signatures and both cover boards. Lay the signatures between the boards and wrap a strip of paper around the work, making sharp creases over the edges (**69**). Use the measurement between creases to lay out the

68

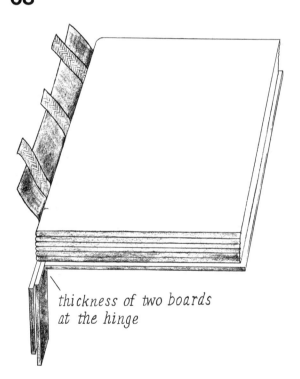

thickness of two boards
at the hinge

width, and make the height the same as the cover boards. Cut the board and slightly round the edges of all three boards with 120-grit sandpaper. A rounded edge makes a better attachment than a sharp one when attaching the cover material.

Attaching boards

With the completion of this operation, in which the tapes and mull are pasted to the insides of the cover boards, the work begins to take on the appearance of a book.

Lay the sewn signatures faceup on the bench. Cut two pieces of waxed paper a little larger than the book and lay them together between the tapes and the mull, pushed well in against the hinge (**70**). Smooth the mull down onto the waxed paper and brush the mull well with paste (**71**). Remove and discard the top sheet of waxed paper, leaving the other clean one in place. Lay the cover board down in position on the pasted mull, and check to see that there is a uniform amount of square on three sides (**72**). Press the board down firmly on the mull, then open the board gently and lay it over on a blank board for support (**73**). Remove and discard the waxed paper. Lay a clean rubbing sheet over the mull and rub it down until completely dry.

Paste down the tapes. Lay a clean piece of wastepaper under the tapes and smooth them out flat (**74**). Then brush them with paste, and paste them again if necessary. Tape usually absorbs more paste than does paper. Pick up the tapes and lay them over onto the mull, making sure they are at right angles to the backbone. Discard the soiled wastepaper and replace it with clean waxed paper. Close the cover board and press it down firmly all along the hinge. After a minute or two of drying, open the cover to check the position of the tapes, then close the cover again and put the work under weights to dry for half an hour.

Remove the weights, open the cover onto a supporting blank board, and trim the tapes

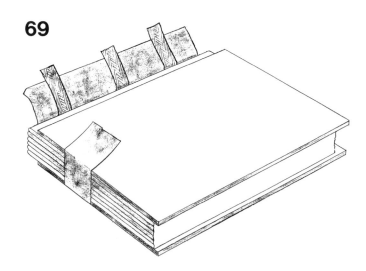

69

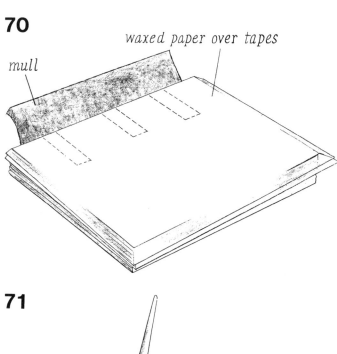

70

mull *waxed paper over tapes*

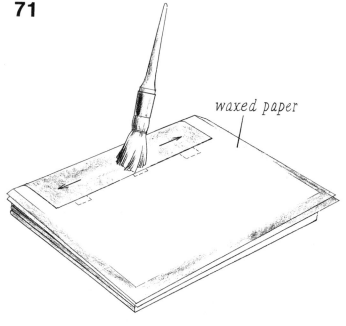

71

waxed paper

72 *cover board in position on pasted mull*

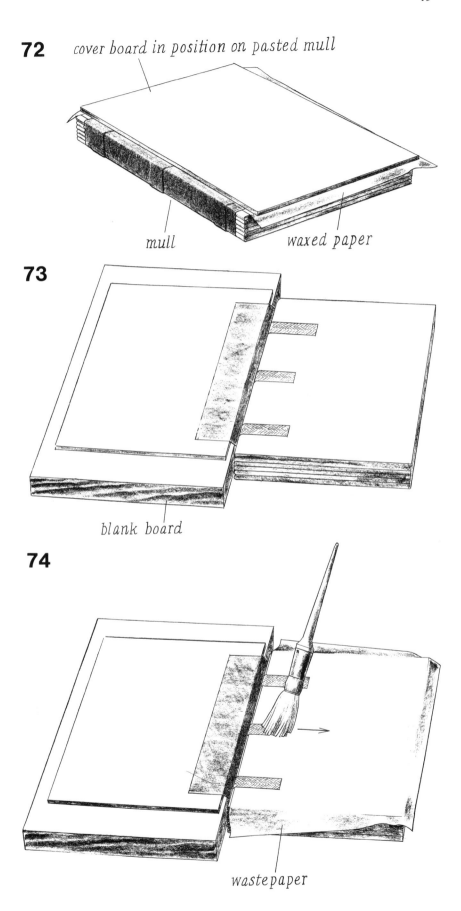

mull

waxed paper

73

blank board

74

wastepaper

and mull (**75**). At the head and foot make pencil marks 1 inch out from the hinge. Align the steel ruler with these marks and make light cuts with a sharp knife. Cut through the tapes and mull only—avoid cutting the board. Peel off the waste, then iron down this new edge with the flat folder. Lay fresh waxed paper inside the cover, close it up, and turn the book over. Attach the back cover board the same way. Then put the work under heavy weights to dry overnight.

75

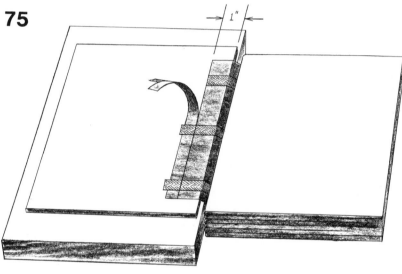

Slitting the mull

When the work is dry, stand the book up with the covers slightly opened. Spread the joint open a bit and use the knife or razor blade to cut a slit about ⅝ inch long down into the mull, holding the knife blade against the edge of the board (**76**). Make two slits at the head and two at the foot, making room to slide the turnovers of the covering material down against the inside of the boards.

Covering the boards

This section describes covering the boards with paper, but the procedure is the same for cloth. Accurate measuring and cutting are important, because any irregularity in the cut edges will show as ridges when the endsheets have been

76

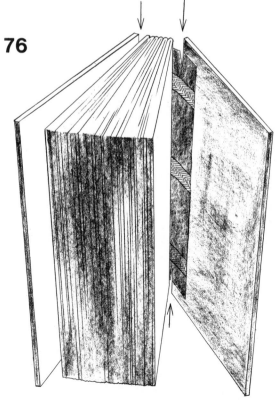

pasted down. And since paper and cloth are easily stained, care should be used in handling and pasting the materials.

Select a sheet of cover paper large enough to more than cover the whole book in one piece. Lay it facedown on the bench. Using the steel ruler, the square, and a sharp pencil, lay out corner marks for all three boards (**77**). Allow a uniform turnover on all four sides and the thickness of two boards for each hinge. A convenient rule is to make the turnovers equal

77 *cover paper*

front   *backbone*   *back*

corner marks   *hinges*   *turnovers*

78

cover paper   *rubbing sheet*

to four thicknesses of board. When the layout is complete, use a sharp knife and the carpenter's square to cut the paper to size.

Attach the backbone board first. Lay it on a sheet of wastepaper and brush it well with paste. Pick up the board and lay it down in position on the cover paper, aligned with the penciled corner marks. Be precise: if this board is attached crookedly, the whole job will be thrown out of alignment. Rub the board down well, then promptly turn the work over, lay a rubbing sheet over it, and with a clean cloth continue rubbing over the backbone until the paste is dry. At the same time gently mold the paper over the edges of the board (**78**).

Next attach the front cover board. Lay the cover paper inside up on the bench, with the

79

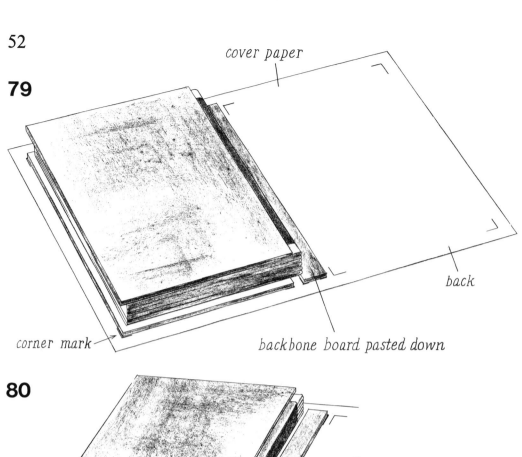

cover paper

back

corner mark

backbone board pasted down

80

81

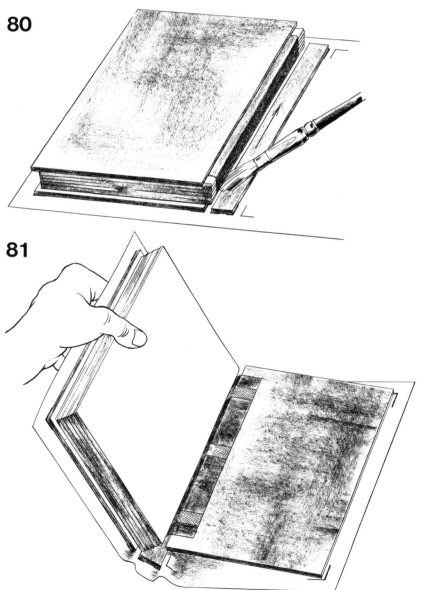

head edge away from you. Brush paste evenly over the front portion of the cover paper, letting the paste run a little beyond the corner marks and sparingly into the hinge. Brush from the center toward the edges. Pick up the book and lay it front-cover down on the pasted paper with the board exactly aligned with the corner marks (**79**). Press down on the book—just to tack it to the paper—then turn the book over. Lay a clean rubbing sheet over the work and rub down with a clean cloth until dry, again working from the center toward the edges to force out any air bubbles.

Attach the back cover board. Lay the work facedown and brush paste evenly over the back portion of the cover paper. Let the paste run a little beyond the corner marks as before, and sparingly into the hinge (**80**). With one hand tip the book up and let the back cover board drop down until it just meets the corner marks (**81**). With the fingers of the other hand, pinch the paper and board together along the edge, then slide the hand under the board to press the pasted paper onto the board. Promptly lay a sheet of waxed paper inside the board, close it up, and rub down the cover paper using a clean cloth over a rubbing sheet. While this paper is still damp, gently crease it over the outside edges of the board, and use the folding stick wrapped in a patch of clean cloth to mold the paper down carefully into the length of both hinges (**82**). Put the work between sheets of clean waxed paper and press for half an hour.

The final stage of covering includes mitering the corners of the cover paper and turning in the head, foot, and fore edges. This work should be done promptly now while the work thus far completed is still a bit damp.

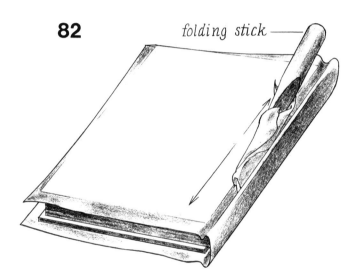

82 *folding stick*

Mitering the corners

Mitering allows neatly finishing the cover paper where it turns over the corners of the boards. In a mitered corner the raw edges of the covering material are folded and hemmed before being stuck down, which in the case of cloth prevents raveling, and in every case makes a more professional job.

The head and foot are turned in first, and the fore edges last. The double thickness of material in a mitered corner necessarily leaves a bulge, which if placed at the foot—the point of greatest friction—soon wears through to leave a blemish (**83**).

Professional corners are not too difficult to make as long as the procedure is carefully fol-

83

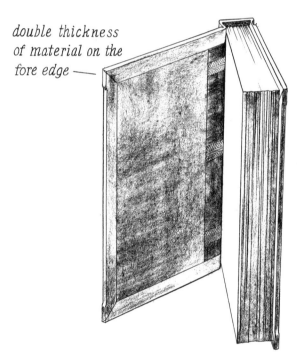

double thickness of material on the fore edge —

84

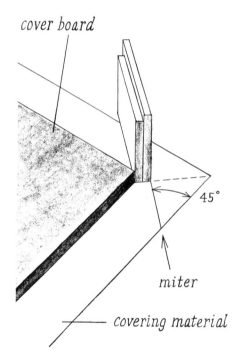

cover board

45°

miter

— *covering material*

lowed. But it is a good idea to make several trial corners in preparation for the finished work. For these trials cut a few pieces of board about 3 × 4 inches, making sure that the corners are square.

The miter is a 45-degree angle cut on a line beyond the corner of the board and at least the thickness of two boards from it (**84**). This allows the extra material needed to make the hem. The 45-degree angles can be measured, marked, and cut individually each time, but a simple mitering jig can be made that will facilitate making uniformly good corners without repetitious measuring.

Lay the book on the bench with the back cover opened onto a blank board for support. Slide a piece of cardboard under the cover. Lay the mitering jig in place on the upper right corner of the cover board. Sighting through the holes in the jig, align the register lines with the edges of the board (**85**). Hold the jig down firmly while you cut the 45-degree angle by sliding the knife or razor along and against the angled corner of the jig. Cut the other miters in the same way.

85

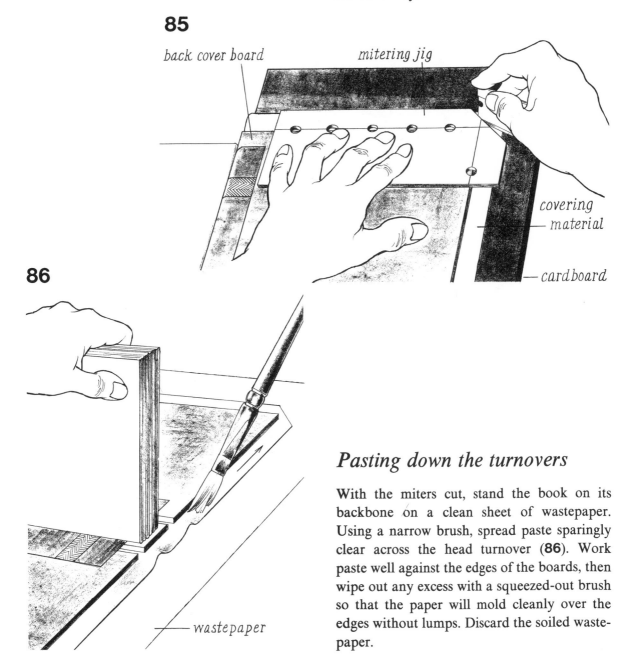

back cover board   mitering jig

covering
material

cardboard

86

wastepaper

Pasting down the turnovers

With the miters cut, stand the book on its backbone on a clean sheet of wastepaper. Using a narrow brush, spread paste sparingly clear across the head turnover (**86**). Work paste well against the edges of the boards, then wipe out any excess with a squeezed-out brush so that the paper will mold cleanly over the edges without lumps. Discard the soiled wastepaper.

87

88

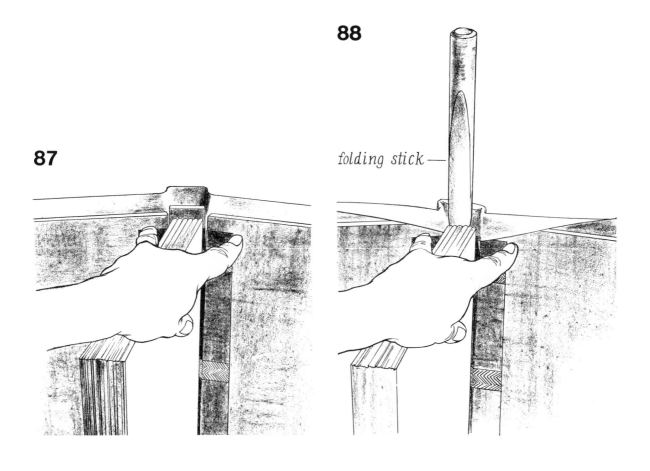

folding stick —

89

folding needle —

90

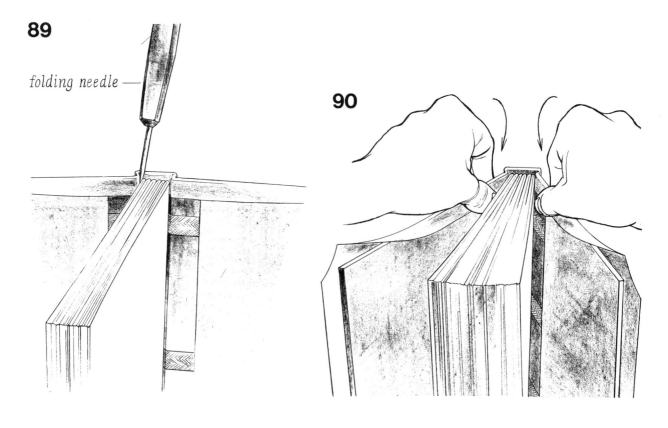

91

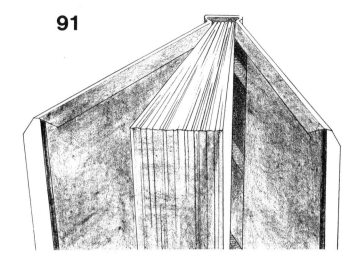

92

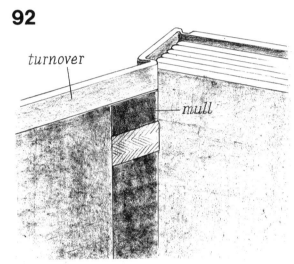

turnover

mull

93

back cover board

wastepaper

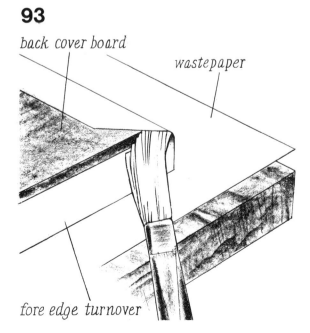

fore edge turnover

Stand the book up with the fore edges toward you, and with one hand hold the covers sprung open (**87**). With the other hand use the end of the folding stick and the folding needle if necessary to tuck the turnover down behind the backs of the signatures and through the slits in the mull (**88, 89**). This section is turned in first. While this appears difficult, it is made easier by manipulating the paper with the thumbs in a rolling, sliding motion, taking advantage of the wet paste as a lubricant (**90**). Continue turning the paper over the edges of the boards, working from the backbone out toward the corners and using the same thumb action to draw the paper tight against the edges of the boards (**91**). Then lay the book on the bench, open one cover at a time onto a blank board for support, and rub the turnovers down well with a clean cloth. Turn the book end for end, stand it up, and use this same method to

94

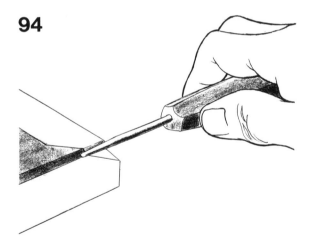

turn in the paper at the foot. Ideally the turnover and the mull should meet in a smooth joint (**92**).

Next turn in the fore edges. Open the back cover and lay it over on a blank board covered with a sheet of wastepaper. With the small brush, touch paste very sparingly inside the pocket of one corner (**93**). Don't leave any excess paste. Iron this pocket down tight against the edge of the board with the folding needle (**94**). With the same brush, lightly paste the

58

corner of the miter (**95**). Pick up the edge of the miter with the folding needle (**96**) and fold it over to make a narrow hem of uniform width (**97**). Iron the hem flat with the folding needle (**98**). Prepare the other corner the same way.

Now brush paste thinly along the whole fore edge turnover (**99**). Work paste against the edge of the board, then wipe out any excess with a squeezed-out brush. At the corner draw

98

95

96

folding needle

97

99

100

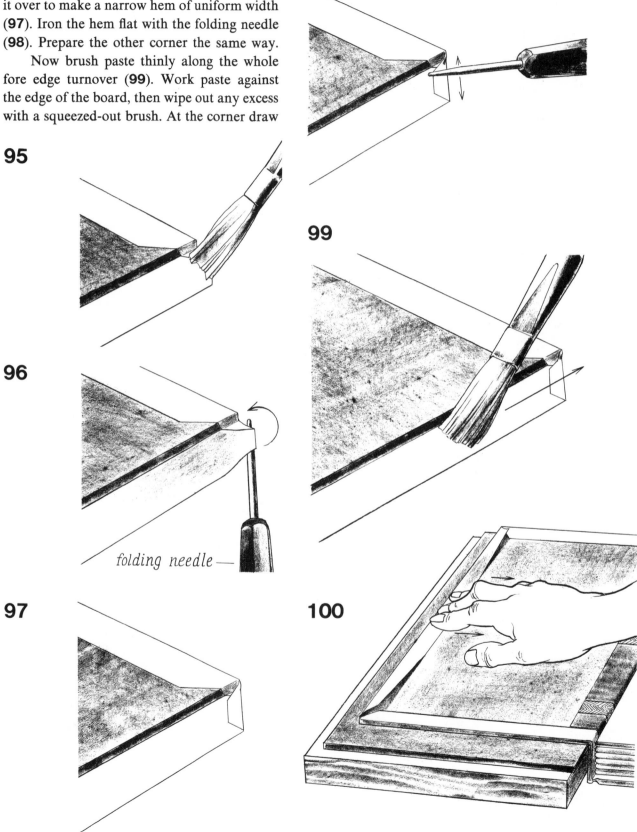

101

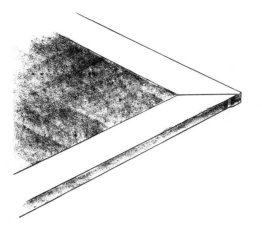

the brush *out across the miter* to avoid a build-up of paste on the exposed edge of the hem. Discard the soiled wastepaper. Slide one hand under the cover and fold the turnover up over the edge of the board. Then, starting in the center of the edge, use the fingers to draw the turnover back tight against the edge of the board (**100**). Continue drawing back the turnover, working from the center toward the corners. Then rub it down well, using a clean cloth over a rubbing sheet. Finally, iron the miters down with the flat folder to make sure they are well stuck. The miters should make accurate 45-degree angles with the inside corners meeting exactly (**101**). If they do not, the fault probably lies in uneven hems (**102**).

Hem the corners of the front cover turnovers and finish it in the same way. Then use the side of the flat folder to tap all four corners slightly blunt (**103**). Lay sheets of waxed paper inside the covers and put under heavy weights to dry overnight.

102

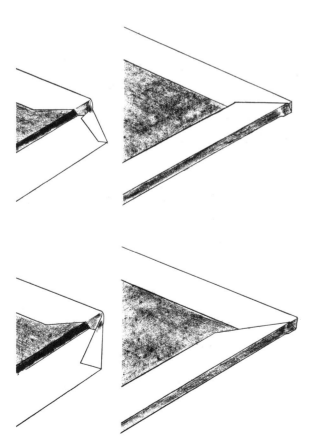

103

Pasting down the endsheets

In this last step in the basic construction of a binding, the first and last leaves of the book—the endsheets—are pasted to the insides of the covers, thus concealing the mull and tapes and the bare surfaces of the boards as well as the edges of the turnovers. This operation also further reinforces the hinges and finishes the book attractively.

Lay the book faceup on the bench with the front cover opened back on a blank board for

104

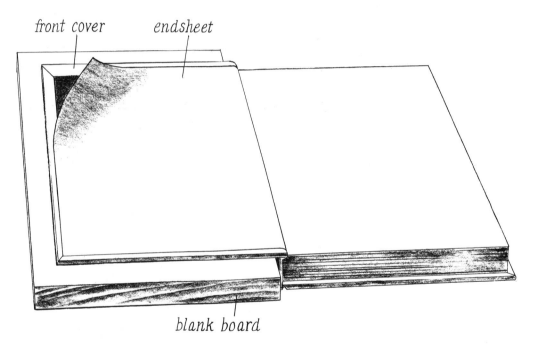

support. Turn the first leaf over onto the cover and smooth it flat (**104**). If the foregoing work has been done accurately, there should be a uniform margin around the three sides of the endsheet, and its corners should exactly strike the seams of the miters. Although at this point it is impractical to correct these margins at the head and foot, a limited amount of trimming can be done on the fore edge. Lay a piece of cardboard under the endsheet and trim the fore edge with a sharp knife or razor blade held against the steel ruler (**105**).

Paste down the endsheet. Slide two sheets

of waxed paper under the endsheet: the top sheet is for pasting and the bottom one is left in place for pressing. Be sure both pieces are pushed tight into the hinge (**106**). Brush the endsheet with a thin, even coat of paste, working toward the edges from the center next to the hinge. Finally, brush a little extra paste along the hinge. Lift the endsheet and discard the soiled waxed paper. Leave the clean one in place. With one hand pick up the edge of the endsheet and pull it out taut with a little tension, while with the other hand you close the

105

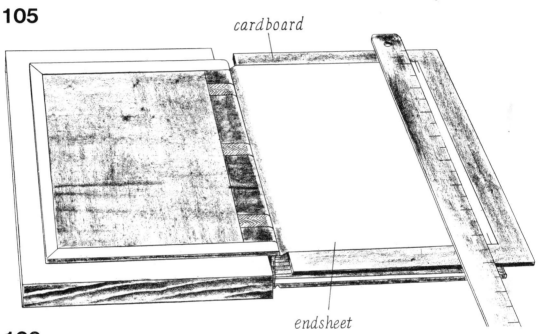

cardboard

endsheet

106

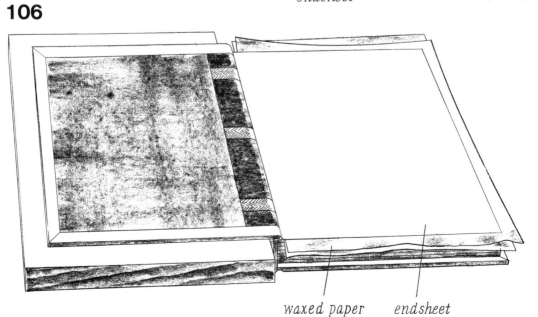

waxed paper   *endsheet*

cover over onto the endsheet (**107**). Immediately open the cover onto the blank board again for inspection. Make certain that the endsheet is smooth along the hinge. If there are wrinkles, promptly pull the endsheet loose and reattach it, this time using a bit more tension as you close the cover. To eliminate air bubbles, lift one corner of the endsheet and smooth it back down, brushing it flat with a clean cloth from the center toward the corners. Then lay a rubbing sheet over the work and rub it down thoroughly, especially along the hinge and around the outside edges. Make sure that the blank board supporting the cover is as thick or thicker than the bulk of the book, and build it up as necessary with sheets of cardboard (**108**). Put clean waxed paper inside the cover, close it, and turn the book over. Paste down the other endsheet the same way. Then put the book under heavy weights to dry overnight.

108

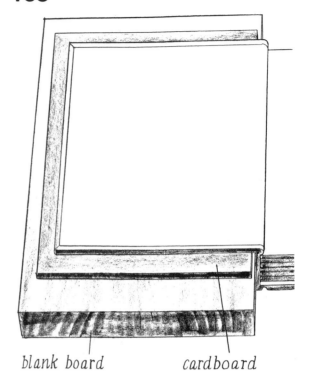

blank board   cardboard

107

waxed paper

Lining the boards

Attaching colored, decorated, or marbled lining papers to the inside of the covers is usually considered a refinement. But linings often serve the more functional purpose of providing additional counter pull to straighten boards unduly warped by particularly heavy covering material.

109

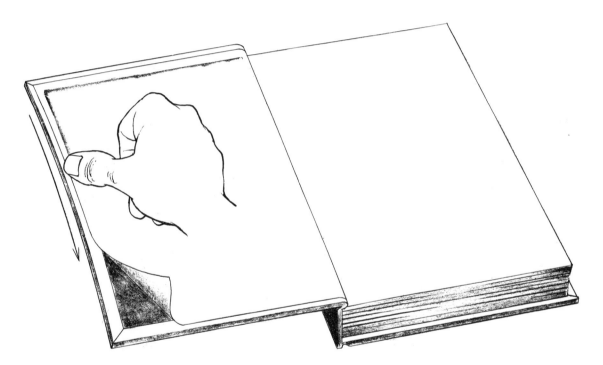

The endsheets are pasted down in the usual way, except that they are first trimmed to fit *inside* the area bordered by the turnovers. To locate the lines for trimming, smooth the endsheet down on the inside of the cover. While holding it firmly in place, use the thumb to iron creases over the edges of the turnovers (**109**). Then slide a sheet of cardboard under the endsheet and trim its edges back to the creased lines. Note that the endsheet must be beveled at the head and foot to make a neat transition over the edge of the board next to the hinge (**110**).

Cut the lining papers to the same size as the book page, then trim off enough more to leave a ⅛-inch margin next to the hinge (**111**). Paste and attach the linings, checking to have uniform margins on the outside edges. Cover with a clean rubbing sheet and rub down until dry. Finally, put sheets of waxed paper inside the covers and press under heavy weights overnight.

110

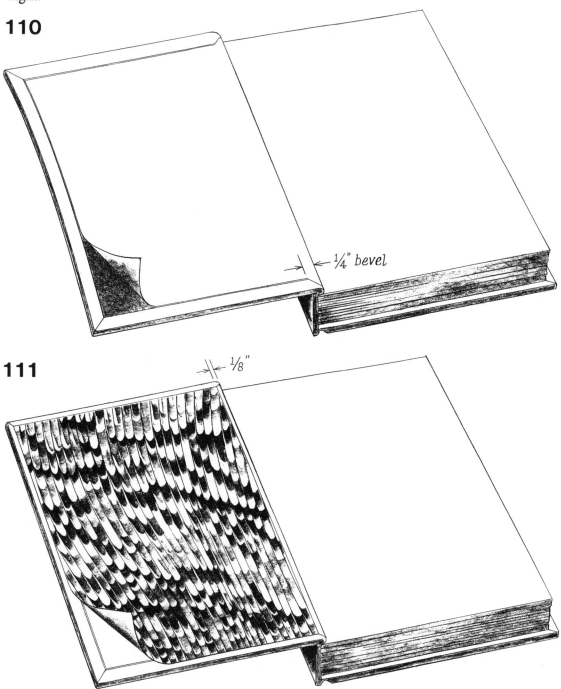

¼" bevel

111

⅛"

5

Binding Projects

This section includes directions for eight binding projects designed to put into practice the procedures described in the preceding pages. Each project opens with an outline and sequence of the procedures required for its completion. When variations or modifications of these steps are called for, they are explained in further detail. The foregoing chapters may be consulted for review of the various technical methods.

1
Dust Jacket

COLORED COVER STOCK, LABEL

Order of Work

SELECT PAPER

MEASURE BOOK

LAY OUT DIMENSIONS

SCORE AND CUT

FOLD UP

MAKE AND ATTACH LABEL

PRESS

112

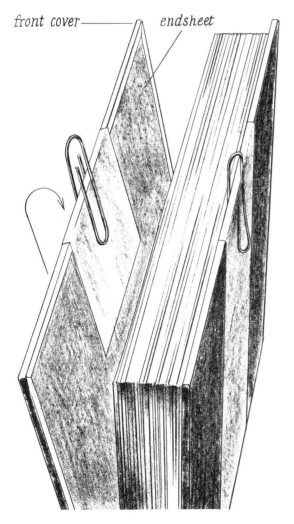

front cover———   *endsheet*

A dust jacket protects the book from dirt, damage, and wear, and in the case of first editions and valuable publications long out of print, preserves the original dust wrapper, paper covers, and binding, and retards further deterioration.

Select a paper whose weight, color, and texture are appropriate to the book to be jacketed. Medium weight paper is usually the most suitable. Thin paper tends to tear at the edges or to cockle with changes in atmospheric conditions. At the other extreme, very heavy papers do not fold as neatly at the hinges and fore edges, often retaining so much stiffness that the jacket flaps will pop the covers open. Cover papers are manufactured in a wide range of plain colors, and the heavier imported handmade papers offer a good choice of patterns, designs, and colors.

First measure the book's wraparound dimension with a strip of paper about two inches wide. Tuck about five inches of the strip inside the back cover, crease it well over the edge of the cover board, and secure it with a paper clip (**112**). Draw it tight, pass it around the backbone, and tuck the loose end inside the front cover. Use a thumb to draw it tight, then hold it in place with another paper clip. Run the fin-

113

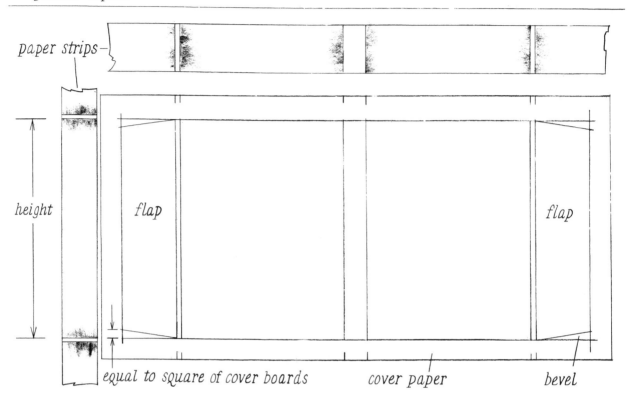

jacket layout

paper strips—

height

flap

flap

equal to square of cover boards   cover paper   bevel

114

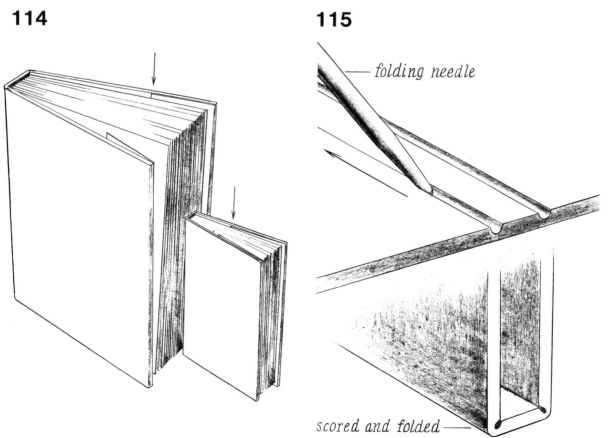

115

folding needle

scored and folded—

116

double-scored

flap

117

single-scored

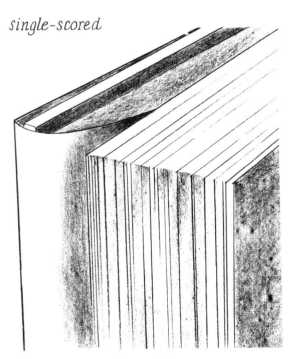

gers along the folds to make good creases at the fore edges and at the backbone. Remove the paper strip. It should have six distinct crease lines from which measurements can be taken (**113**). Use another paper strip to measure the height of the book. Note that a dust jacket extends from the head to the foot with no overhang.

On a sheet of cover paper a bit larger than the finished jacket, lay out the dimensions on the wrong side of the paper. Transfer the measurements from the paper strips by stretching them out flat and making pencil marks on the layout opposite each crease line (**113**). Make the flaps about one-third the width of the book cover. For a small book the flaps should be wider to prevent them from popping the covers open (**114**). Lay out the flap bevels to conform to the square of the book (**113**).

Scoring

Scoring, which should always be done on the inside of the fold, compresses the paper, actually reducing its thickness along the fold line (**115**). This ensures a straight fold, but more important, it allows the paper to fold without breaking the fibers and leaving whiskers visible along the outside edge of the fold.

It is especially important to double-score the jacket at the fore edges to conform to the thickness of the cover boards (**116**). A jacket with single-scored fore edges pulls away from the covers and forces them open (**117**). Before scoring the finished jacket, make a few trials on scraps of the paper you will use, to gauge the angle of the folding needle and the amount of pressure required.

Score all six folds on the inside of the jacket with the work laid facedown on a sheet of smooth, hard cardboard. Score clear across the paper and beyond the finished edges of the jacket. Align the steel ruler or the carpenter's square with corresponding pairs of pencil guide marks. Hold the ruler in place as tightly as possible and maintain the pressure while

118

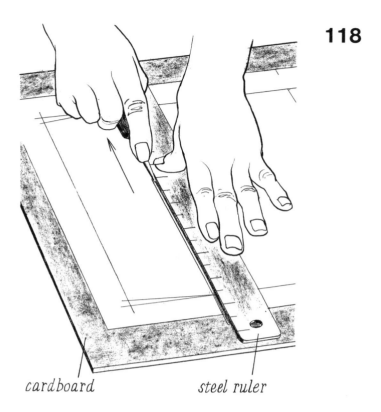

cardboard   steel ruler

119

folding sequence

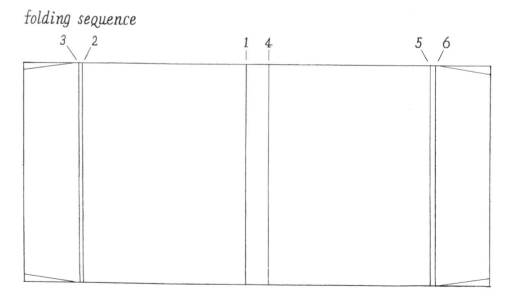

you use the folding needle held at a flat angle, drawing it alongside the ruler in a steady, one-shot stroke (**118**).

Trim the jacket to exact size. Lay the marked-out and scored cover paper on the sheet of cardboard, and use the square and a sharp knife to trim all four sides to the pencil guidelines. Hold the square down firmly, and make two or three light cuts rather than one heavy one. Do not cut the bevels on the flaps—they are trimmed later.

Folding

With the jacket facedown on the cardboard, fold up the scored lines in the sequence shown in the diagram (**119**). Align the ruler exactly on the scored line and hold it down as tightly as possible with one hand. With the other pick up the paper and fold it up against the edge of the ruler (**120**). Without moving the ruler, run the fingertips along the fold, pressing the paper tight against the edge of the ruler to make a decisive crease. Remove the ruler and *lightly* crease the paper partway down on itself, but do not use the flat folder here, as too sharp a crease may crackle the paper. When folding lines 3 and 6, bear down on the ruler with all the pressure possible to prevent the paper from sliding under the ruler and spoiling the narrow double fold.

Finally, lay the jacket faceup on the cardboard and cut the bevels on the flaps, starting the cuts a fraction beyond the outer folds of the fore edges. Clean off the pencil guide marks with a soft eraser. Make and attach the label. Put the jacket on the book, cover it with waxed paper, and put under weights to dry.

120

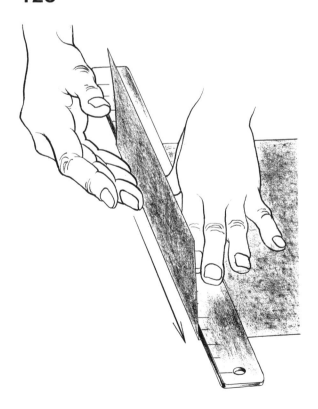

121

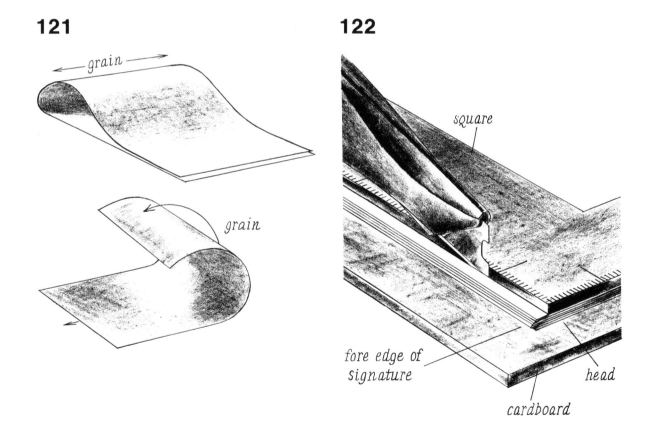

grain

grain

122

square

fore edge of
signature

head

cardboard

2
Blank Book
Single Signature

PAPER COVERS, SEWN AND TIED

Order of Work

CUT AND FOLD SIGNATURE PAPER

CUT COVER PAPER

COLLATE

MARK UP AND SEW

FOLD UP COVER

MAKE AND ATTACH LABEL

PRESS

123

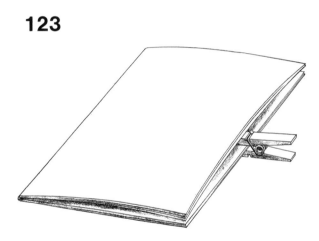

Select signature paper and test it for *grain:* For the leaves of the book to turn easily, the paper should be cut so that the fold runs in the same direction as the grain of the paper. To test, lay a sheet on the bench and roll it back on itself. If the sheet droops down flat, the grain is parallel to the rolled edge. And if it arches up, the grain is at right angles to the edge (**121**).

Cut six sheets 9 × 12 inches, to be folded into a 6 × 9-inch signature. Measure accurately and use the carpenter's square when cutting. Fold the six sheets as one unit. Pick up all the sheets and jog them gently on the bench to align them. Fold and make a firm crease with the flat folder. Use only moderate pressure to avoid rippling the folded edge.

Lay the signature on cardboard on the bench with the head edges away from you, and trim the fore edge as follows: Align one arm of the square even with the head edges of the signature and the other arm just back of the fore edge (**122**). Hold the square down as firmly as possible, and use a sharp knife held snug against the edge of the square. Make several light cuts with moderate pressure, holding the knife in the same position for each stroke.

Heavy pressure on the knife will cockle the paper. After trimming, clip a clothespin over the back half of the signature to hold the alignment, and lay it aside (**123**).

Next cut the covers. Lay out a cutting diagram on the inside of a sheet of medium weight paper, using the steel ruler, the carpenter's square, and a sharp pencil. Allow a square of ⅛ inch at the head and foot, and 2½ inches for each flap. Make a single score for the center fold only, using the steel ruler and folding needle. Trim the covers to size, following the pencil guidelines. Then fold up and lightly crease the center fold. Leave the flaps as they are; they are scored and folded after sewing.

Collate the work. Lay the signature inside the folded covers, adjusting it so there is a uni-

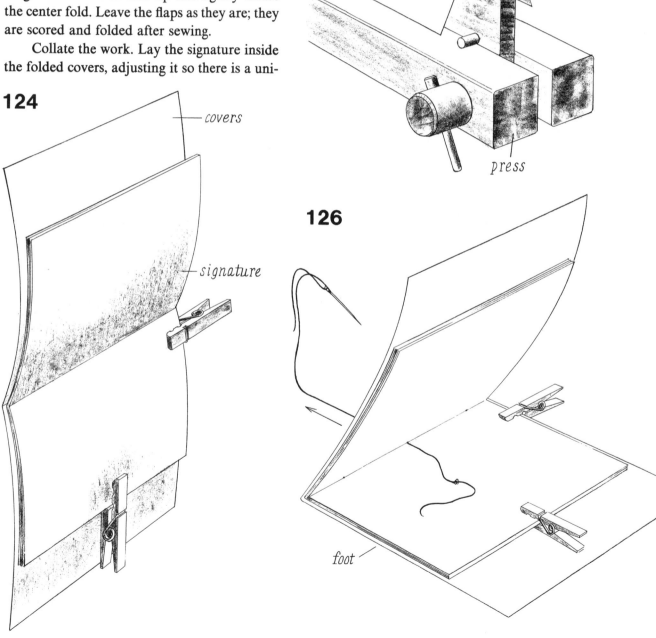

125

piercing board

press

124

— *covers*

— *signature*

126

foot

form square at the head and foot. Clip another clothespin over the work close to the fold, to hold the alignment (**124**).

Mark up for piercing and sewing. Pick up the signature and covers—leave the clothespins in place—and put them over the piercing board (**125**). On the folded edge (backbone) of the covers, make a pencil mark at the center, another mark 1¾ inches down from the head, and a third mark 1¾ inches from the foot. Pierce a hole at each pencil mark, clear through the covers and the signature. Leave the clothespins in place.

Sew up the book. Thread a needle with a 30-inch length of thread, wax it, and tie a knot in the loose end, leaving a 4-inch tail. Remove the work from the piercing board and lay it flat on the bench with the foot of the signature toward you. Open the signature at the center and slide one hand inside to hold it open. The signature and covers are sewn as one. Starting at the center hole, take the needle from the inside to the outside (**126**). Draw the thread through

127

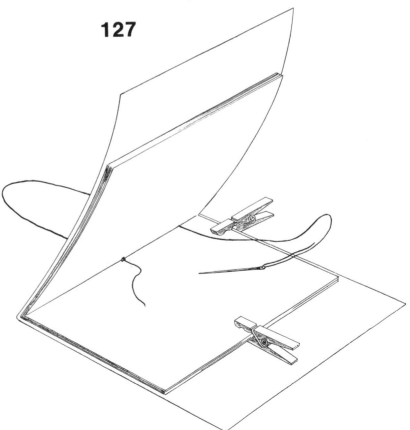

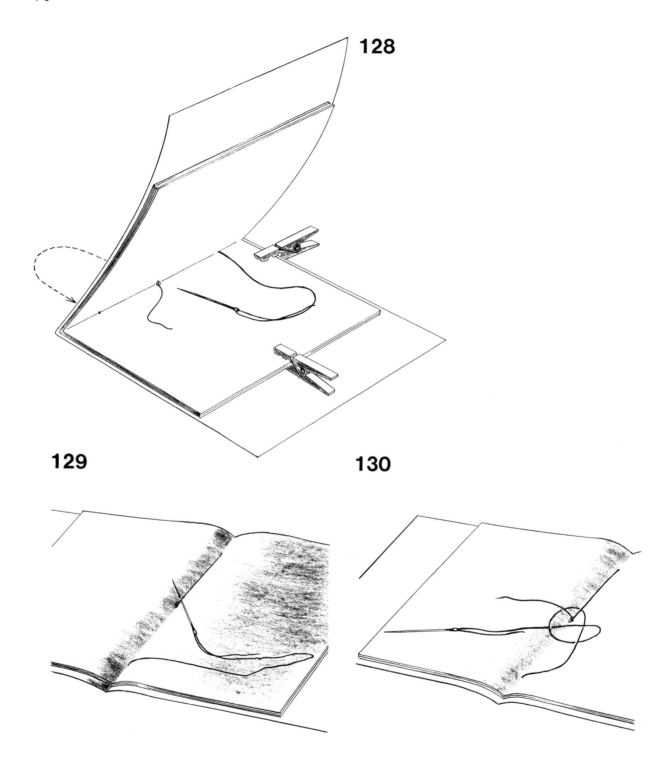

128

129

130

and snug against the knot, then push the needle in at the head hole and draw the thread up snug (**127**). Now take the needle out through the center hole again (**128**). Then take the needle in at the foot hole and draw the thread snug. Tie the thread to the center knot by sliding the needle under the thread beyond the

131

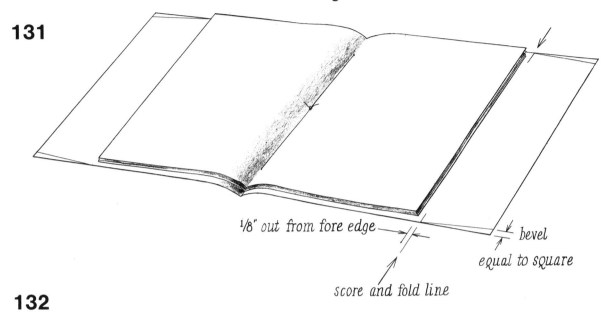

1/8" out from fore edge

bevel
equal to square

score and fold line

132

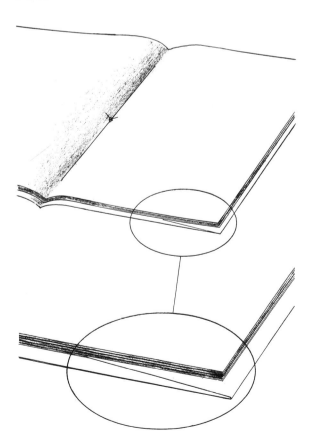

knot and throwing a loop around under the knot (**129**). Finish tying off by passing the needle through the loop and drawing the thread into a tight knot (**130**). Trim off the tails to within 1/4 inch of the knot.

To finish the flaps first measure out 1/8 inch from the fore edge of the signature and make a single scored line from head to foot on each flap (**131**). Then cut bevels on the head and foot of each flap. Fold up the flaps. Tuck them inside the endsheets and close the book (**132**).

Make and attach the label. Put the book under weights until the label is dry.

3
Folio

PAPER-COVERED BOARDS,
FULL LINING

Order of Work

MAKE BOARDS

CUT COVER PAPER

ATTACH BOARDS

MITER CORNERS

PASTE DOWN TURNOVERS

CUT LINING PAPER

ATTACH LINING

MAKE AND ATTACH LABEL

PRESS

A folio makes a useful protective case in which to store single and odd-size items such as press clippings, catalogs, type specimen booklets, photographs, drawings, or letters. The rigid covers maintain the contents flat, and by excluding light retard their becoming discolored or brittle.

Cut two medium-weight cover boards 6¼ × 9½ inches, and a backbone board measuring ½ × 9½ inches. Slightly round the edges of all three boards with fine sandpaper held over a wooden block.

Select a sheet of cover paper. Lay it facedown on the bench and draw corner marks to position all three boards. Allow a ½-inch turnover on all four sides, and the thickness of two boards for each hinge. Cut the cover paper to exact size, according to the pencil guide marks.

Attach the front cover board. Lay the cover paper facedown on the bench on a sheet of wastepaper. Spread paste over the front-cover portion of the paper, letting the paste run a little beyond the corner marks. Lay the cover board down in position on the pasted paper, making sure that it is aligned with the corner marks. Press down on the board to tack it in place, then immediately turn the work over. With a clean rubbing sheet over the work, rub the paper down well on the board, working from the center toward the edges to force out any air bubbles. Cover the work with waxed paper and put under heavy weights to dry for half an hour.

Attach the remaining boards. Brush paste evenly over the back-cover portion of the paper and the backbone area as well. Lay the backbone board down in alignment with the corner marks, and lay the back cover board in position as well. Press the boards down firmly, then turn the work over and rub the paper down well, as before. Leave the work flat, cover it with waxed paper, and put under heavy weights to dry for half an hour.

Miter the four corners of the paper, then paste and turn in the head and foot turnovers. Paste and turn in the fore edges. Lay a rubbing sheet over the work and rub the turnovers down thoroughly to make sure their edges are well stuck. Cover the work with waxed paper and a sheet of cardboard, and put under heavy weights to dry overnight.

Make and attach the lining. Select an appropriate paper, giving some thought to the overall color scheme. If the boards have been covered with a solid color paper, a decorative lining makes an agreeable contrast, while a plain white or buff lining would harmonize with a patterned cover.

Lay the flat folio on the bench and use strips of paper to measure for a one-piece lining. Allow a 3/16-inch margin around all four sides, and be sure to crease the paper strip well down into the hinges to get an accurate measurement of the width (**133**). Then cut the lining paper to size.

To attach the lining, paste the whole sheet, brushing from the center toward the edges. Pick up the lining and lay its left-hand edge in position on the front cover board, checking the margins. Hold the rest of the lining clear with

133

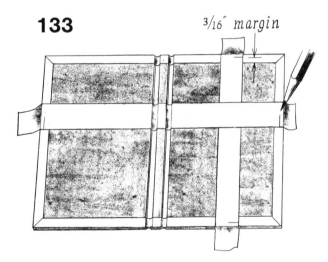

3/16" margin

one hand (**134**). Gently rub down the extreme left-hand edge to tack it in place. Still holding the lining up under a little tension, smooth the paper down onto the front cover board, then use the thumb or a finger to work it down into the hinge (**135**). Continue attaching the paper from left to right, across the backbone board and into the other hinge. The remaining paper can now be smoothed down across the back cover board. Cover the work with a rubbing sheet and rub down all the surfaces until they

134

135

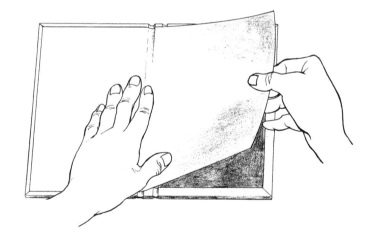

are free of air bubbles and firmly attached. Make sure that the edges are well stuck.

Close up the folio over a blank board built up if necessary with pieces of cardboard to the full thickness of the backbone. While the paper is still damp, gently mold both hinges with the edge of the folding stick wrapped in a clean cloth.

Make and attach the label. Then lay sheets of cardboard either side of the folio just back of the hinges to prevent crushing them. Put the work under heavy weights to dry overnight.

4
Blank Book
Four Signatures

CLOTH BACK, PAPER SIDES

Order of Work

CUT AND FOLD SIGNATURE PAPER

MARK UP AND SEW ON TAPES

SQUARE THE BACK AND HEAD

ATTACH THE MULL

MAKE AND ATTACH BOARDS

ATTACH CLOTH BACKBONE

MAKE AND ATTACH PAPER SIDES

PASTE DOWN ENDSHEETS

MAKE AND ATTACH LABEL

PRESS

136

deckle edge

This binding has many practical uses and because of its solid construction is superior to commercially made blank books marketed as sketch books and notebooks. Another advantage in making your own blank books is that the paper can be selected exactly to suit a specific purpose. Among the wide range of papers available are those manufactured especially for pen and ink, charcoal, watercolor, and calligraphy, and writing papers in an assortment of colors, textures, and finishes.

If the paper you are using has a deckle, or feather, edge, arrange to cut and fold it so that the deckle falls at the foot of the page (**136**). The head edges should be smooth to minimize dust accumulation, and it is practical as well for the fore edges to be smooth and even to permit easy turning of the pages.

Cut thirty-two sheets 9 × 12 inches to be folded into four signatures of eight sheets each measuring 6 × 9 inches. The number of sheets can be varied according to the weight of the particular paper. If the paper is thinner than 20-pound typewriter, add two or three sheets (before folding) to each signature, and reduce the number for heavy papers such as charcoal and pen-and-ink drawing paper.

Pick up four sheets at a time—or enough for one signature—jog their head edges even, then fold up as one unit. Mark this signature with the number 1 at the foot next to the fold. Fold and sign the other signatures (**137**).

Gather up all the signatures and jog their heads lightly on the bench. Lay them on the bench and use the squared card to align the head and the back.

137

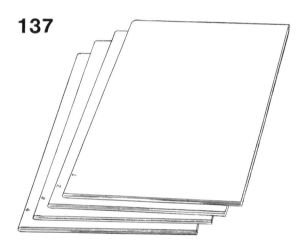

Mark up for sewing on two ½-inch tapes, locating the tapes to balance the weight of the signatures (**138**). Pierce the holes, then set up the sewing frame. Thread and wax a 30-inch length of thread and knot the free end, leaving a 2-inch tail beyond the knot. Sew up the signatures. Remove the sewn signatures from the frame and paste together the first and last pairs of signatures along their extreme back edges to prevent their gaping open.

Cut a piece of mull 1 inch shorter than the height of the signatures and 2½ inches wider than their bulk combined with the two cover boards. Tape waxed paper to the jaws of the press. Put the signatures in the press with their backs about ½ inch above its jaws. Check again to be sure the signatures are flat across the back

138

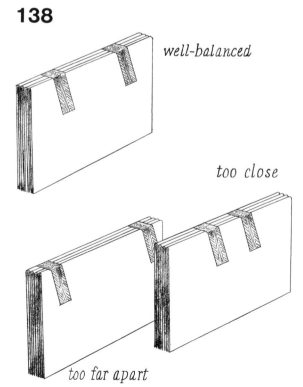

well-balanced

too close

too far apart

139

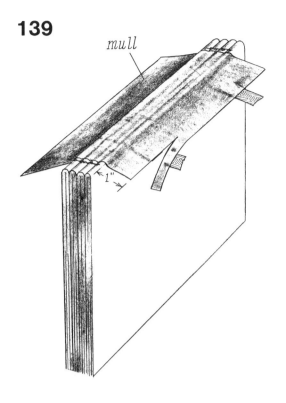

mull

1"

and square at the head, then tighten the press. Paste and attach the mull. When it has dried, trim the mull and tapes back to within 1 inch of the hinges (**139**).

Make and attach the boards. Allow a square of ⅛ inch around three sides and the thickness of two boards for each hinge. Make the width of the backbone the same as the bulk of the signatures and both boards combined. Then attach the boards, slit the mull at the head and foot, and put the book in the press with its backbone about 3 inches above the press jaws.

In this binding a cloth strip covers the backbone, extends across the hinges, and is attached to the outside of the cover boards. Before cutting the cloth, keep in mind that inside the covers of any binding, the edges of the mull, tapes, and turnovers—and in this binding the turnovers of the cloth back and paper side panels—will be very conspicuous even after the endsheets have been pasted down over them (**140**).

For all these pieces to align neatly, the width of the cloth back must be gauged as accurately as possible. Lay one cover board and the backbone board on the sewn signatures so

140

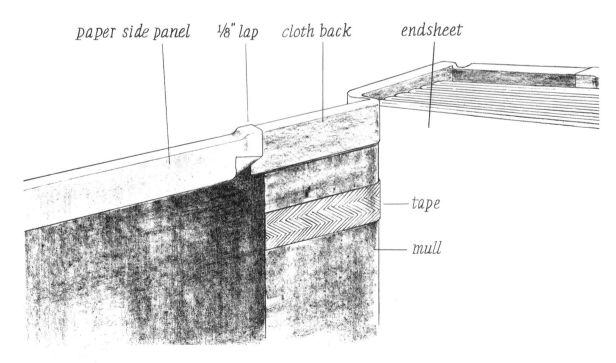

paper side panel *⅛" lap* *cloth back* *endsheet*

tape

mull

that one end of the mull is showing (**141**).
Tape a strip of paper to the backbone and
smooth it over onto the cover board. With a
finger rub the paper well down into the hinge,
then make a pencil mark in line with the edge
of the mull. Make another mark ⅛ inch outside
the first. The correct width of the cloth back is
two times the distance AB in the illustration,
plus the width of the backbone board.

141

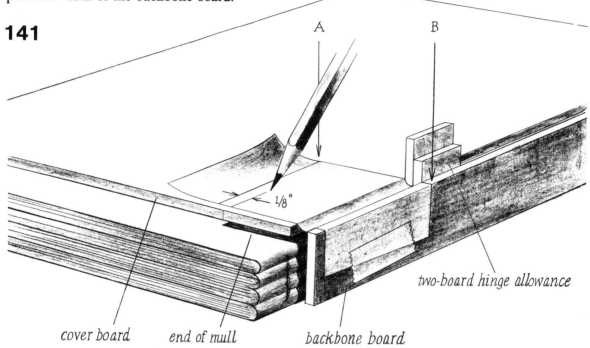

width of cloth back = 2x distance AB plus width of backbone board

142

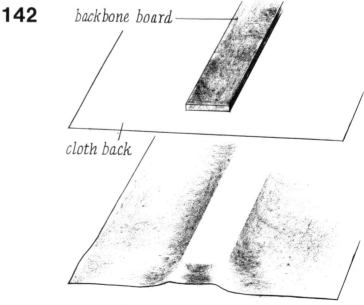

creased over edges of board

Cut the cloth, making sure that the weave runs parallel with its length. Paste the backbone board and brush paste as well onto the cloth, then attach the board to the cloth strip centered in both directions (**142**). Turn the work over and rub it down well, creasing the cloth slightly over the edges of the board.

To attach this board-and-cloth unit to the book, paste the cloth either side of the backbone board. Paste the edges of the board, but wipe out any excess with a dry brush to eliminate lumps. Lay the pasted unit down onto the back of the book (**143**), and adjust its position

143

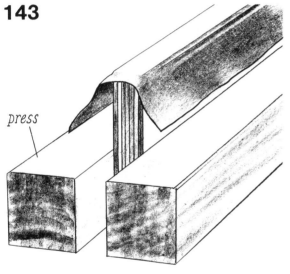

144

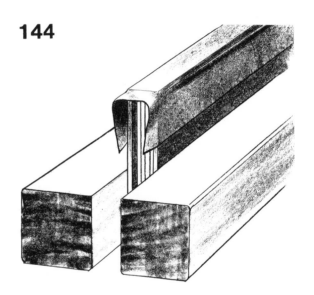

145

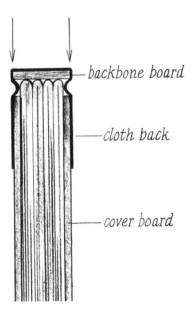

backbone board

cloth back

cover board

so that all three boards are aligned at the head and foot. Pinch the cloth along the edges of the backbone board and down into the hinges. Then smooth the cloth down against the cover boards and press it against them to hold things in place temporarily (**144**). Looking at the edge of the book, check to see that the edges of the backbone board are flush with the cover boards (**145**).

Promptly take the work out of the press, lay it flat on the bench, and crease the cloth down into one hinge. Flop the book over and crease in the other hinge. Then rub down the cloth on both covers, using a clean cloth over a rubbing sheet. The rubbing sheet is especially important here, as otherwise the cloth tends to slide on the wet paste and creep out of position.

Stand the book up with the covers opened partway, and use the folding stick and folding needle to turn in the cloth at the head and to work it down against the insides of the boards (**146**). Then turn the book end for end and turn in the cloth at the foot. Again mold the cloth into the hinges with the folding stick wrapped in a clean cloth. Put sheets of waxed paper inside both covers and over their out-

146

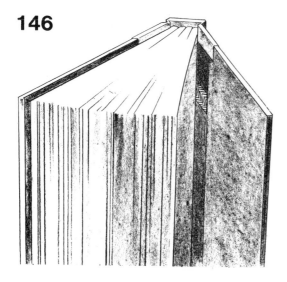

sides, and put the book under heavy weights to dry overnight.

Make the paper side panels, measuring and cutting each one individually, as the dimensions of the cover boards may not be precisely identical. Allow an amount of turnover at the head and foot that will align with the cloth back just turned in, and enough width so that the paper side panels lap over the cloth ⅛ inch (**147**). Paste and attach the side panels, miter their corners, and paste down the turnovers. Then paste down the endsheets.

Make a final inspection to see that all the paper edges are well stuck, especially where they lap over the cloth. Blunt the corners of the cover boards by tapping them with the side of the flat folder. Make and attach the label. Cover the book with waxed paper and put under heavy weights to dry overnight.

147

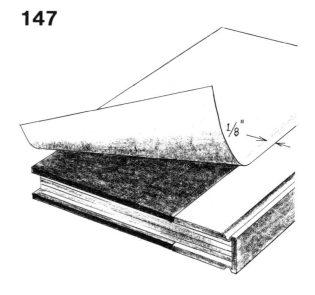

5
Blank Book Scrapbook

A scrapbook is made as described in Project 4 but requires the additional work of removing every other leaf to create *stubs* that will compensate for the bulk of the papers, photographs, or other materials to be inserted.

Lay the finished blank book on the bench, opened to the center of the first signature (**148**). Slide a piece of hard cardboard under the next leaf, pushed in snug against the sewing. At the head and foot measure out ⅜ inch from the sewing and make light pencil marks. Align the steel ruler with these marks and trim out the leaf. Remove the cardboard, turn the next leaf, and replace the cardboard under the leaf following. Trim out this leaf the same way. Continue cutting out every other leaf, but stop when you reach the center of the last signature. The uncut portions of the first and last signatures are necessary to ensure strength in the sewing.

148

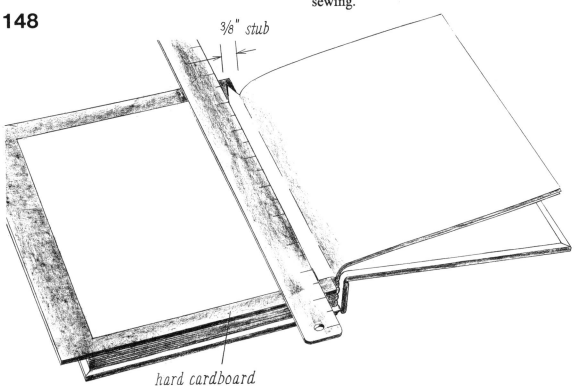

⅜" stub

hard cardboard

149

front sheets   *back sheets*

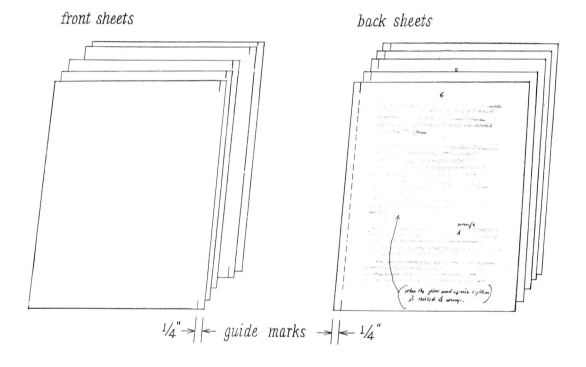

¼" →| |← *guide marks* →| |← ¼"

6
Manuscript Binding

SINGLE SIGNATURE, CASE BINDING

Order of Work

GUARD THE SHEETS

MAKE ENDSHEETS

COLLATE

FOLD UP SIGNATURE

SEW UP ON TAPES AND MULL

TRIM FORE EDGE

150

back sheets

guide mark

In this style of binding single sheets of a manuscript are *guarded,* or pasted together edge over edge in pairs to create the fold necessary for sewing. The sheets in the front half of the manuscript are attached to the edges of corresponding sheets of the back half, then folded as a single signature.

Assuming that the manuscript consists of ten sheets, separate the sheets into two sections. Lay the first five sheets facedown on the bench and the last five faceup (**149**). On the back of each of the front sheets make light pencil guide marks at the head and foot ¼ inch from the right-hand edge. Make similar marks on the face of the back sheets ¼ inch from the left-hand edge. The back sheets will be trimmed to these marks (shown in the illustration as a dotted line). The front sheets are not trimmed. Pick up the back sheets and jog them to align their edges. Lay them on the bench with the head edges toward you. Lay the carpenter's square on the sheets, one arm aligned with the head edges and the other aligned with the ¼-inch guide marks (**150**). Hold the square down tight while you trim the sheets with a sharp knife, making several light strokes with moderate pressure.

Paste the sheets together in pairs, beginning with the first front sheet and the last back sheet. Lay the front sheet facedown on a piece of wastepaper. Lay a piece of straight-edged wastepaper on the manuscript sheet in exact alignment with the ¼-inch guide marks (**151**). Hold the wastepaper firmly to prevent it from slipping while you brush paste *sparingly* along the exposed edge of the manuscript sheet. Brush from left to right across the edge. Discard all the soiled wastepaper and lay the work

151

first front sheet

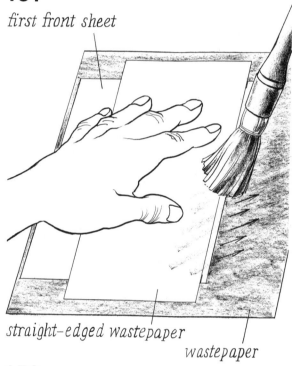

straight-edged wastepaper

wastepaper

152

last sheet of manuscript

10

guide mark

pasted edge

on a clean piece. Pick up the last back sheet of manuscript—faceup—and lay it on the sheet just pasted, being careful to align its left-hand edge with the ¼-inch guide marks (**152**). Lay a clean rubbing sheet over the work and rub it down well. Set the pasted sheets aside under waxed paper and a sheet of cardboard with weights on top. Continue pasting up the remaining pairs of sheets in the same way, using a fresh piece of straight-edged wastepaper each

153

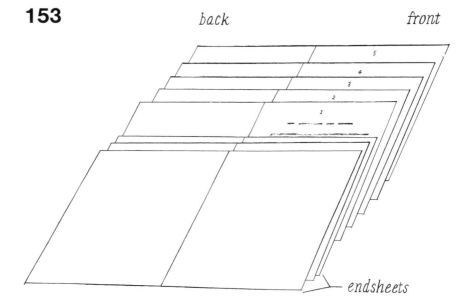

back   front

endsheets

time, and stacking them between pieces of waxed paper under the weighted cardboard to dry completely.

Extra pages are now added to provide endsheets for pasting down and for blanks at the front and back of the manuscript. Prepare six sheets of typewriter paper as described, trimming and pasting them together as flat double sheets.

Collate the work. Lay the manuscript sheets faceup on the bench with the endsheets on top, fanned out to verify their correct sequence (**153**). Then pick up all the sheets, jog them both ways into alignment, and fold them up as a single signature.

Note that in this binding the mull goes *under the tapes* and is sewn to the signature along with them. Cut a piece of mull 3½ inches wide and 1 inch shorter than the height of the signature. Fold and crease it lengthwise down the center, using the flat folder. Put the signature over the piercing board and lay the creased mull on top, centered head to foot (**154**). Mark up for two ½-inch tapes, and pierce six holes through the mull and the signature—four for the tapes and two for kettlestitches. Thread a needle with a 30-inch length of thread, wax the thread, and knot the free end, leaving a 3-inch tail. Set up the sewing frame. Start sewing at the foot. Take the needle in at the foot kettlestitch hole, out at the next, then over the tape and in again at the hole above it. Sew in and out to the head (**155**). Draw the thread up snug, then sew in and out again through the same holes to the foot. Draw the thread snug, and tie a knot under the starting knot. Trim the tails off to within ¼ inch of the knot.

Trim the mull and tapes back on both sides to a width of 1 inch (**156**). Put the work under a blank board and heavy weights to compact the fold. It is now ready for attachment to the case, the making of which is described in the next section.

155

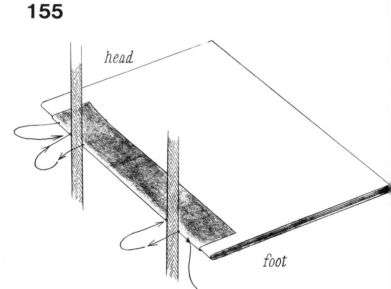

154

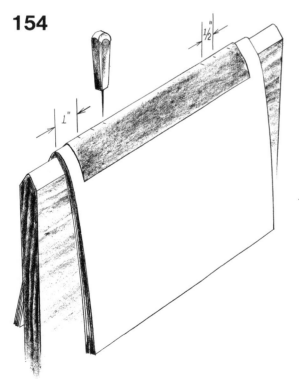

156

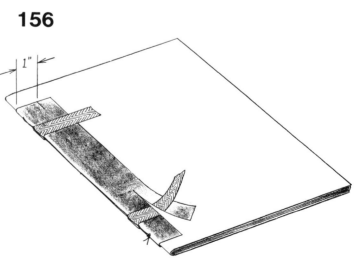

7
Square Back Case

PAPER-COVERED BOARDS

Order of Work

MAKE BOARDS
CUT COVER PAPER
ATTACH BOARDS
MITER CORNERS
PASTE TURNOVERS
ATTACH CASE TO SIGNATURE
PASTE DOWN ENDSHEETS
MAKE AND ATTACH LABEL
PRESS

157

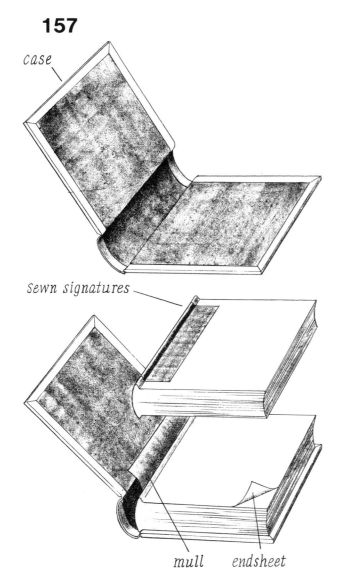

case

sewn signatures

mull *endsheet*

Machine-made books are almost always case-bound. The covers and backbone—the case—are fabricated as a separate unit and then attached to the sewn signatures, which are also manufactured separately (**157**). Rarely sewn on tapes, such books are reinforced with only a lightweight mull glued to the backs of the signatures. Therefore, because the mull and pasted-down endsheets are the only means by which the signatures and the case are joined, this type of binding has limited strength and durability. The hand binder can improve on the case binding, however, by sewing onto tapes, using a heavier mull, and when there is only a single signature, by sewing tapes and mull in the same operation, as described in Project 6.

First make the cover boards, allowing a square of ⅛ inch at the head, foot, and fore edge, and the thickness of two boards for each hinge. Slightly round their edges with fine sandpaper. Then lay the signature between the boards to measure the total bulk with a strip of paper (**158**). Use this measurement to lay out and cut the backbone board. Sand its edges slightly round.

Use another strip of paper to measure clear around the book. Set the backbone board in place against the back of the signature and clamp everything together with a taped band of paper (**159**). Tuck one end of the measuring strip inside the cover board, crease it well over the edge, then wrap the strip clear around and inside the other cover board. Crease all the edges well, working the paper down into the hinges.

Transfer these measurements to the wrong side of a sheet of covering paper. Lay the boards on the cover paper and locate their position with penciled corner marks. Allow a ½-inch turnover all around and the thickness of two boards for each hinge (**160**). Then cut the paper to size.

Paste the three boards and attach them to the cover paper, starting with the backbone board. Keep the corners aligned with the penciled corner marks. As each board is attached, turn the work over and rub the paper down well, creasing the paper slightly over the edges of the board. Protect the case with waxed paper and lay it flat under a blank board and heavy weights to dry overnight.

Cut corner miters on the paper and paste

158

159

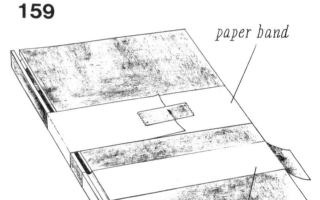

paper band

measuring strip

160

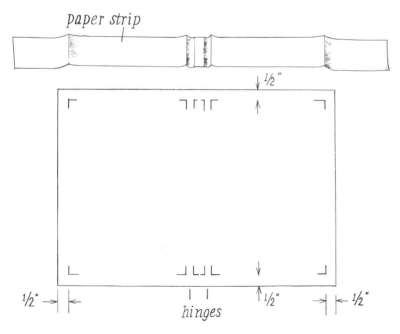

paper strip

½"

½"

hinges

½"

½"

down the turnovers, working the head and foot first, followed by the fore edges. Close the case over a blank board, and mold the paper down into the hinges with the edge of the folding stick wrapped in clean cloth. Leave the blank board in place, cover the work with waxed paper, and put under heavy weights to dry overnight.

Attach the case to the signature. Lay a sheet of wastepaper on the signature under the mull and tapes, paste the mull, then press the tapes down on the mull. Paste the mull and tapes again, working paste well into the weave (**161**). Discard the soiled wastepaper and replace it with a sheet of waxed paper. Pick up the signature and lay it down on the inside of the back cover. Hold the signature by the unpasted front portion of the mull, lowering it into position as you align the square around the edges of the board (**162**). Lay a blank board over the unpasted mull, put heavy weights on top, and leave the work to dry for a few minutes. Then turn the signature over to the left, lay a clean rubbing sheet over the pasted-down mull, and rub it down well. Discard the rubbing sheet and replace it with waxed paper. Turn the signature back in place

161

wastepaper

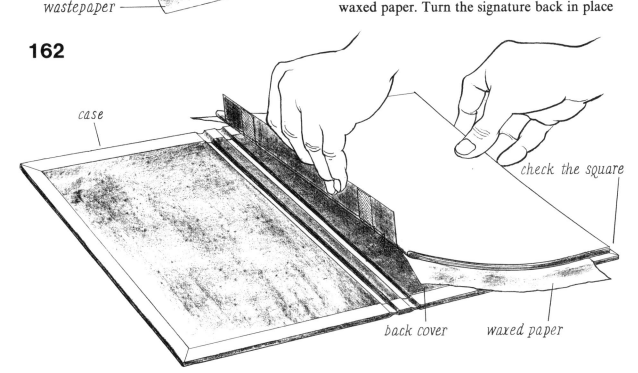

162

case

check the square

back cover   waxed paper

and lay a cardboard and weights on top. Leave the work to dry for an hour.

To attach the front board of the case, slide a sheet of wastepaper under the mull and paste the mull and tapes as before (**163**). Discard the soiled wastepaper and replace it with waxed paper. With the narrow brush sparingly paste inside both hinges. Close the front cover over onto the pasted mull. Stand the right-angle card against the backbone to make sure it is square to the bench (**164**). Press down on the front cover over the mull to tack it in place. Then open the cover onto a supporting blank board and rub the pasted mull down as before. Put clean waxed paper inside the cover, protect the work with a clean rubbing sheet and a blank board, and lay heavy weights on top. Leave the work to dry for an hour or more.

Remove the weights and mold the paper down into the hinges, using the edge of the folding stick wrapped in clean cloth. Paste down the endsheets. Lay clean waxed paper inside both covers and put the work under heavy weights to dry overnight. Make and attach the label, finally putting the book under weights again to dry thoroughly.

163

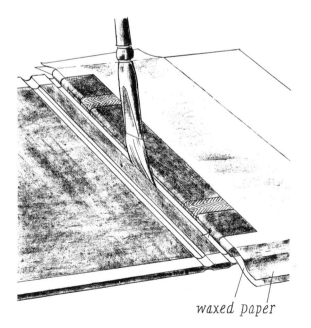

waxed paper

164

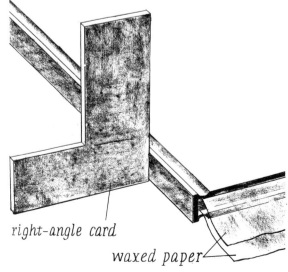

right-angle card

waxed paper

8
Music Binding

CLOTH BACK, PAPER SIDES

Order of Work

GUARD THE SHEETS

MAKE ENDSHEETS

COLLATE

CUT THE MULL

MARK UP AND SEW

MAKE AND ATTACH BOARDS

CUT AND ATTACH CLOTH BACK

MAKE AND ATTACH PAPER SIDES

PASTE DOWN ENDSHEETS

MAKE AND ATTACH LABEL

PRESS

165

salvaging the title panel

Damaged music books and sheets can be repaired and their utility extended in a simple binding that will last almost indefinitely. Wear typically occurs in three places: along the folded back edge of the covers and pages, at the top outside corners as a result of having been folded down to facilitate turning the pages, and in the center fold of the book, which frequently pulls loose from the staples.

Preparatory to sewing up as a single signature, repairs are made on the covers and inside pages by guarding with patches or strips of new paper pasted over the damaged portions. In extreme cases when all the pages have come loose as single sheets, guarding also means reattaching them in pairs for folding, as described in Project 6. If the original covers are too far gone to repair, cut out and salvage the panel that carries the title and other information, and paste-mount it as a label on the new cover (**165**).

For the strongest job guard all the folded sheets—not just the obvious ones—and both sides of the center ones where the staples were clinched. This provides a solid foundation for the new sewing. Make the guards from a thin but durable high-quality rag-content writing paper, matching the color as closely as possible to that of the music. If the damage is within the area of the printed music itself, then use a thin, transparent silk fabric.

Begin by taking the music apart. Carefully remove the staples, brush out all dirt, and gently clean off as much of the rust deposit as

166

wastepaper   *cardboard*

167   *guard strip and wastepaper trimmed flush*

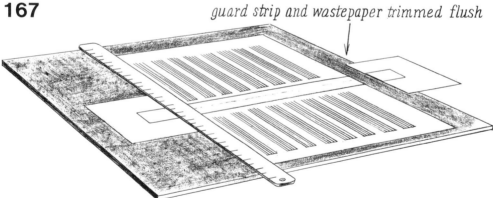

can be practically done with a soft eraser. As each sheet is removed, sign it with a number to be used in collating, then lay it aside flat and faceup on the bench.

Cut guard strips ¾ inch wide and about 3 inches longer than the height of the music sheet. Starting with the center pair of pages, smooth them out flat on a sheet of cardboard, with wastepaper under the music. Paste a guard strip, then pick it up in both hands. Hold

168

it a bit taut to keep it flat and straight (**166**). Without letting it droop, lower it onto the music, centered over the fold line. Press the thumbs down to tack the guard to both the music and the wastepaper. This holds the work from slipping. Then lay a rubbing sheet over the work and rub the guard strip down dry. Trim the guard even with the head and foot of the music, using the shears or a sharp knife and the steel ruler (**167**). Turn the work over and guard the reverse side the same way. This extra layer of paper allows the sewing to be drawn up very firmly without thread tear-out. Guard the remaining pairs of sheets the same way, but on the inside only.

Dog-eared or broken corners should be mended with patches of new paper extending a bit beyond the actual damage (**168**). Make the patch large enough to cover the repair and reach well out beyond the corner of the page (**169**). Lay the music flat on wastepaper over a sheet of cardboard. Paste the patch and lay it in

169

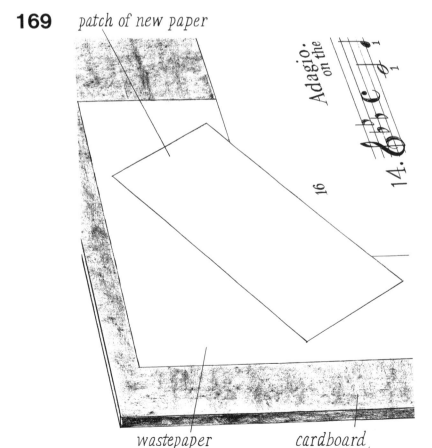

patch of new paper

wastepaper   *cardboard*

position over the damage. Put a clean rubbing sheet over the work and rub the patch down well. Discard the rubbing sheet. Trim the patch and the wastepaper even with the original corner of the music (**170**). As the sheets are guarded and mended, stack them facedown flat on the bench between sheets of waxed paper. Lay a sheet of cardboard and weights on top.

Make four endsheets from similar paper, cutting two sheets to be folded to the size of the music. Collate the endsheets with the music, jog their top edges on the bench to align them, and fold up as a single signature. Clip a clothespin over the head of the signature to hold the alignment.

Cut a piece of mull 2 inches wide and 1 inch shorter than the height of the signature. Fold and crease it lengthwise with the flat folder. Put the signature on the piercing board and lay the creased mull over it, centered to give uniform margins at the head and the foot (**171**).

Mark up for piercing, locating one mark an inch from the head, another mark an inch from the foot, and three additional marks evenly spaced between. Pierce the holes through the mull and signature.

Thread a needle with a 30-inch length of thread, wax the thread, and knot the free end, leaving a 3-inch tail. Transfer the work to the sewing frame and slide one hand inside the center of the signature to hold it open. Starting at the foot hole, take the needle in through the mull, out through the next hole, and draw the thread up snug against the knot. Then sew in and out clear to the head. Draw the thread snug, then sew in and out through the same holes back to the foot. Draw the thread up snug and tie a knot under the starting knot. Trim off the tails to within ¼ inch of the knot.

Cut two cover boards the same height as the music—with no square, or overhang—to facilitate catching and turning the pages. Measure their width to the same as the music less ¼ inch for each hinge. Slightly round the edges of the boards with fine sandpaper.

170

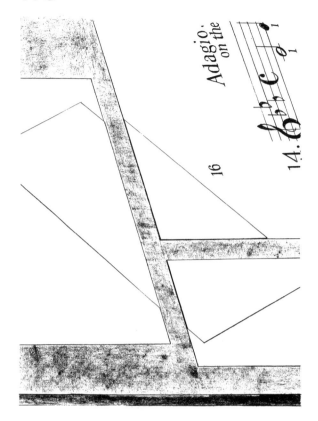

171

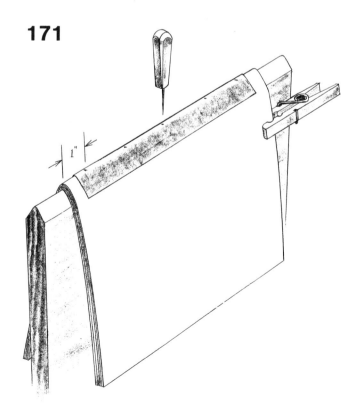

172

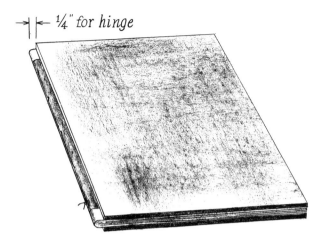

←| ¼" *for hinge*

Paste the mull and attach the boards to it, making sure that their edges are flush with the signature at the head, foot, and fore edge (**172**). Lay waxed paper inside both boards and put the work under heavy weights to dry overnight.

Cut a piece of cloth for the backbone, 3 inches wide and 1 inch longer than the height of the boards. Put the book between blank boards in the press, leaving the backbone projecting 2 or 3 inches above the press. Fold and crease the cloth lengthwise. Paste the cloth well and lay it over the back of the signature, with an equal amount of overhang at the head and foot (**173**). With the fingers, pinch the cloth along the back of the signature and down into firm contact with the boards. Use a clean rag to rub the cloth down until it is well stuck.

Remove the book from the press and stand it up with the fore edge facing you and the covers spread open. Use the small brush to replenish the paste on the inside of the cloth turnover. Use the folding needle to tuck in the

173

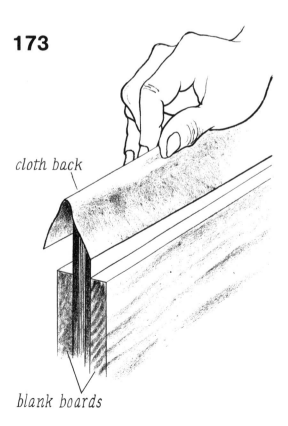

cloth back

blank boards

cloth at the head, drawing it down with the thumbs to form a neat cap and to stick it to the boards (**174**). This takes some patience, because the turnover is actually stuck to itself. Turn the book end for end and turn in the foot the same way, repasting the cloth as before to ensure good adhesion.

Make the paper sides, allowing a ½-inch turnover at the head, foot, and fore edge, and a ⅛-inch lap over the edge of the cloth back (**175**). Paste and attach the sides, rubbing them down well, especially where they lap over the cloth. Miter the corners and paste down the turnovers, working the head and foot first, followed by the fore edge. Put the work under weights to dry for an hour. Then paste down the endsheets. Press under heavy weights to dry overnight. Make and attach the label.

174

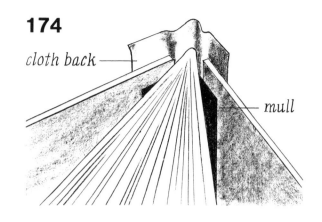

cloth back

mull

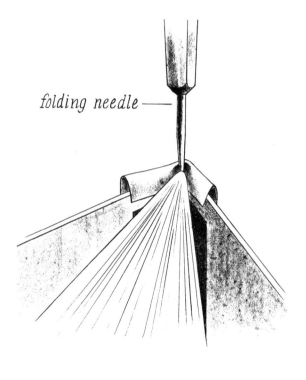

folding needle

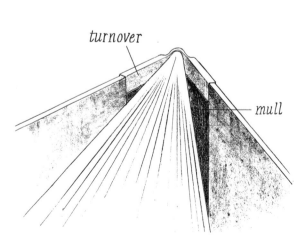

turnover

mull

175

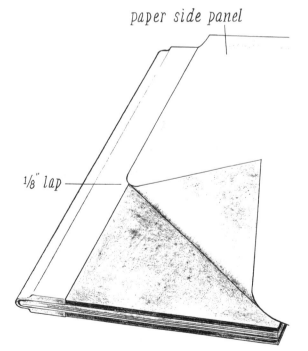

paper side panel

⅛" lap

6

Rebinding an Old Book

Order of Work

TEAR APART

KNOCK OUT GROOVES

REPAIR DAMAGE

MARK UP FOR SEWING

KNOCK DOWN SWELLING

ROUND AND BACK

MAKE HOLLOW BACK

176

paperbacks

sewn signatures

perfect binding

An immediately practical use of hand binding is the repair of valuable but seriously worn or damaged books. Whether originally published as hardcovers or paperbacks, they can be rebound in the traditional way as long as they were manufactured with folded and sewn signatures. Books originally made as perfect bindings, however, cannot practically be rebound (**176**). In a perfect binding the printed and folded signatures are guillotine-trimmed on all four sides—eliminating altogether the folded backs of the signatures. The spine or backbone is then mechanically roughened, and a flexible adhesive is forced into the roughened back edges of the pages, which are now single leaves. Theoretically the single leaves could be guarded and restored as folded signatures, but the enormous swelling produced by the thickness of so much extra paper could never be taken up by rounding and backing. Although both hardcover and paperback books are quite commonly perfect-bound, their life expectancy is dramatically shorter than that of a book with a sewn binding. And the hardcover version offers little advantage other than the deceptive appearance of strength, since all that holds the book together is a thin strip of mull and a band of adhesive.

Whereas the square back binding is appropriate for a relatively slender book (**177**), the considerable bulk of a book with ten or fifteen signatures or more must be given a round back to compensate for the swelling created by the numerous threads lying inside the signatures (**178**). A by-product of rounding the back is the formation of shoulders into which the cover boards are fitted (**179**).

178

177

179

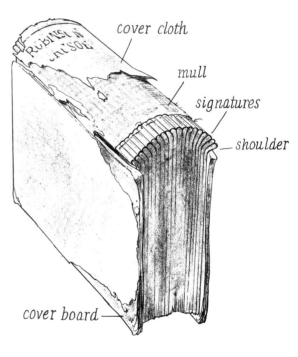

180

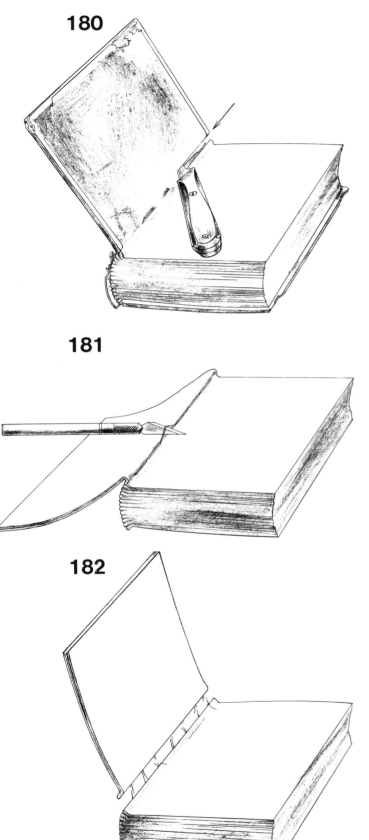

181

182

Tearing apart

Before a book can be rebound, its covers, mull, and sewing must be removed. This is called *tearing apart,* a term that implies rough handling but that in fact calls for great care to prevent damaging the signatures, especially on their insides next to the sewing.

Lay the book faceup on the bench and open the front cover. With a sharp knife slit along the hinge, cutting through the endsheet, the mull, and the cover cloth (**180**). Be careful not to cut into the paper of the first signature. Next, open the book to the center of the first signature to expose the old sewing. Ease the knife under the loops of thread, turn the knife edge-up, and cut the threads (**181**). Cut loose all the threads in this signature the same way. Lift the signature out and lay it facedown on the bench (**182**). If it does not come loose readily, do not yank it with sudden pressure. Slit the mull between the two signatures, remove the first signature, then use the fingers to work loose any particles of dried glue around the sewing. Go to the center of the next signature and repeat the process. Continue tearing apart all the signatures. Pick out the remnants of old thread—inside and out—then collate the signatures by referring to the numbers or bars (sometimes both) printed on their back edges (**183**). Of course, if the signatures are not signed, number them in sequence as you tear the book apart.

183

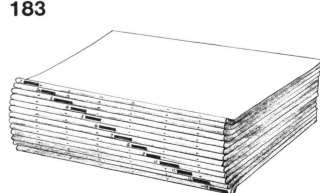

Knocking out the groove

This means flattening the groove, or bend, along the edge of the signatures (**184**). To ensure that the new sewing—and consequently the entire binding—will be as tight and solid as possible, all the old grooves must be knocked out and the signatures restored as nearly as possible to a flat condition. Note that the signatures next to the boards have more pronounced grooves than those in the center of the book and will therefore require more work.

184

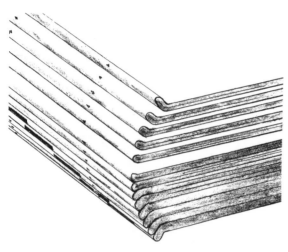

185

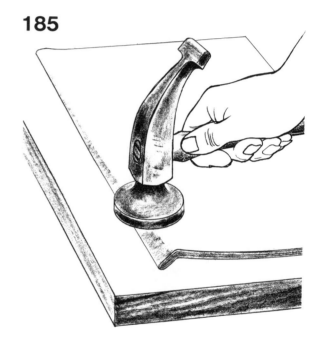

Knock out the grooves individually. Lay a signature groove-down on a flat piece of hardwood such as a blank board. Holding the backing hammer up close to the head, gently tap along the groove, striking the face of the hammer flat to avoid denting or bruising the paper (**185**). Work all along the signature and back again, using many overlapping light strokes rather than heavy blows. As a signature is finished, lay it on the bench under a board and heavy weights to help hold it flat.

Repairing damage

After knocking out the grooves, go through and examine the signatures for damage. Repair weak or torn corners and guard the signatures as needed, especially their center folds, as described on pages 89–91 and 97–100.

Marking up for sewing

In marking up an old book for sewing, it is essential for the sake of strength to pierce new holes, keeping well clear of the old ones, even if the tapes and kettlestitches must be located unsymmetrically (**186**).

186

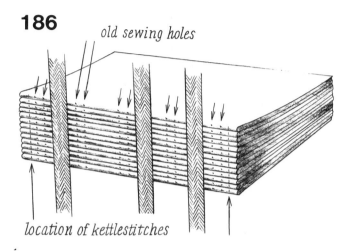

old sewing holes

location of kettlestitches

Knocking down the swelling

After sewing a book with more than just a few signatures, there is a noticeable swelling at the back (**187**). Some of this is caused by the signatures springing open despite the grooves

187

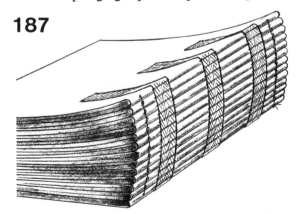

having been knocked down. But more of it is due to the numerous threads lying inside the folds of the signatures, a condition that is exaggerated when heavier thread is used. Although rounding and backing will take up most of this swelling, knocking down the swelling immediately after sewing helps compact and improve the solidity of the work.

Lay the sewn signatures on a hardwood board and place a piece of thick cardboard or plywood on top, just back of the start of the swelling (**188**). Square up the backs of the signatures so that they are one above the other. Hold the work in this position, with one hand bearing down on the cardboard. Using the hammer in the other hand, knock down the swelling by working along the edge of the book and back again. Use good firm strokes but keep the hammer face striking flat to avoid damaging the paper. After each two or three passes along the back edge, realign the backs of the

188

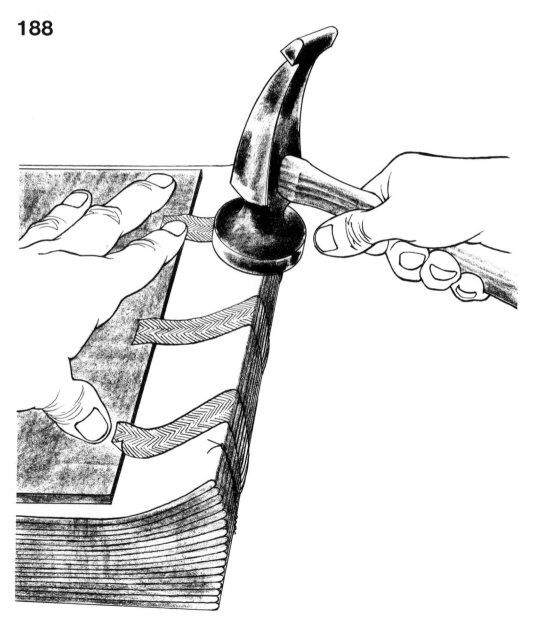

189

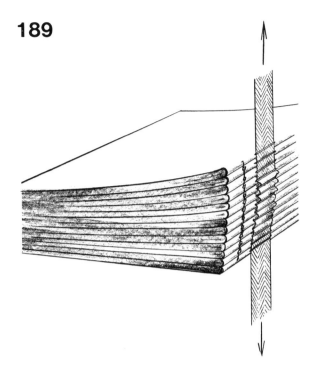

signatures one above the other. Then turn the book over and knock down the swelling from the other side. Finally, pull the tapes out taut from both sides to eliminate the puckering between the sewing threads (**189**).

Rounding

Preparatory to backing, the back of the book is now given an even, rounded shape. Lay the book on a backing board on the bench, overhanging the edge of the board ½ inch or so. Manipulate the signatures into a moderately round shape, using both hands to achieve a uniformity from the head of the book to the foot (**190**). The face of the backing hammer is often useful here to gently tap the signatures into place while some finger pressure is being applied. The degree to which the back is rounded, of course, depends on the number of signatures and the total bulk of the book. Too much round cannot be worked into good shoulders, and too little prevents taking up all the swelling.

190

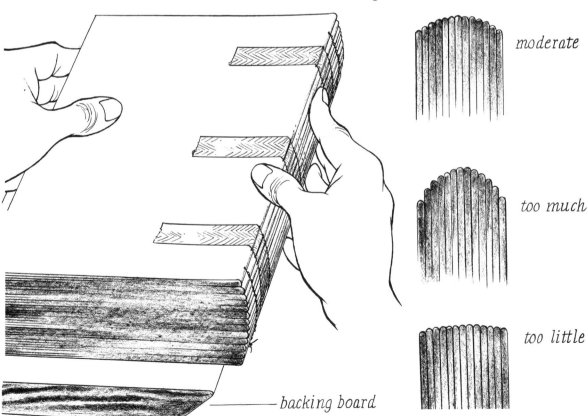

moderate

too much

too little

backing board

Without shucking the book out of shape, lay the other backing board on top and put the work in the press (**191**). Tighten the press a bit, then adjust the book so that the outside signatures project above the bevels of the backing boards an amount equal to the thickness of the cover board to be used. Check the contour of the rounded back again, correcting any irregularities by loosening the press enough to work the signatures from underneath as well as on top. Then tighten the press, turning the screws alternately to maintain even pressure.

191

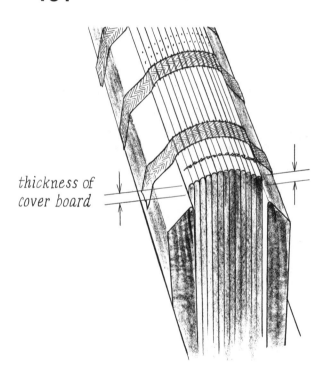

thickness of
cover board

192

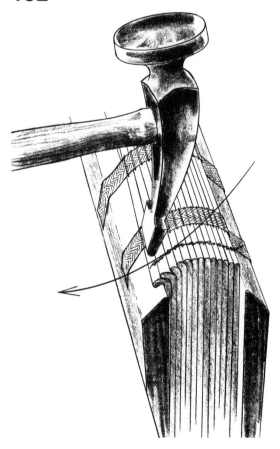

Backing

With the book secured in the press, use the backing hammer to gently tease the signatures from the center toward the sides to form shoulders along the hinges. Standing at the long side of the press, use light, glancing hammer strokes—tapping, pulling, and bending the signatures away from the center toward the shoulders (**192**). Backing should be done gradually.

Attempting to hurry the process means using heavy strokes and the probability of mashing, rather than bending and drawing, the signatures. Work slowly back and forth along the back of the book and alternately from both sides to keep the shape symmetrical. The claw of the hammer is designed especially for this job, but see that it strikes evenly along its full width, or its corners may tear the signature paper and strain the sewing. Once the backing is well under way, the face of the hammer can be used advantageously to smooth the contour.

As shown in the illustration (**193**), the center signature has no bend, or groove, while those on either side are turned over progressively deeper to develop the shoulders to the full width. The outside signatures can be backed well down over the beveled edges of the backing boards. While this appears to give the shoulders an exaggerated angle, they will straighten out as the paper naturally springs back afterward.

The back of the book can now be pasted and the mull attached while the work is still in the press, but first tape strips of wastepaper along the top edges of the backing boards to protect them from the paste.

Making a hollow back

In a *tight back* leather binding, the leather is pasted directly to the backs of the signatures, so that the backbone and the leather flex as one when the book is opened and closed. In *hollow back* construction, generally used when the book is covered with more fragile material such as cloth or paper, a tube of paper is built up on the backbone of the book. One side of the tube is pasted to the mull over the backs of the signatures, and the other side to the covering material. This allows the book itself to open and close without bending and damaging the covering material.

To make a hollow back, put the book backbone-up in the press (**194**) and measure the bulk (including covers) with a strip of

193

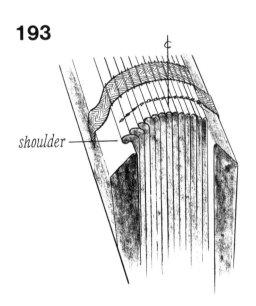

shoulder

194

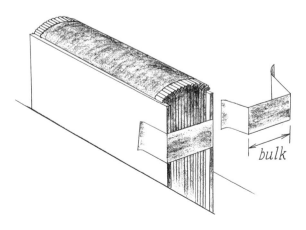

bulk

paper. Use this dimension to lay out and cut a piece of heavy kraft paper 1 inch longer than the height of the cover boards and three times the measured bulk.

Fold and crease the paper into thirds lengthwise. Spread paste on the backbone of the book, working it well into the mull and the backs of the signatures. Lay panel A of the kraft paper on the pasted backbone, centered in both directions (**195**). Rub it down well with a clean cloth until dry.

Lay a piece of wastepaper over panel A, and fold panel B down on top of it (**196**). Paste

195

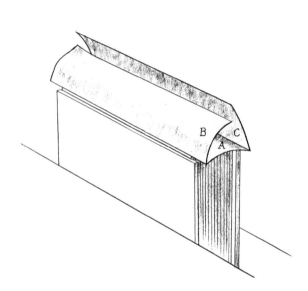

196

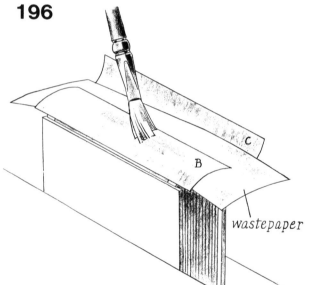

wastepaper

197

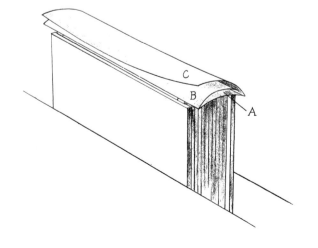

panel B; remove and discard the soiled wastepaper. Fold panel C back over on top of the pasted panel B and rub it down until it is well stuck and dry (**197**).

Trim the hollow back even with the cover boards at the head and foot (**198**). Then slit both sides between panels A and B at the head and foot to make room for turning in the cover material. Finally, open the covers partway and use a small pair of pointed scissors to carefully trim the waste paper of panel A flush with the signatures at the head and foot.

198

trimmed even with cover boards

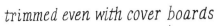

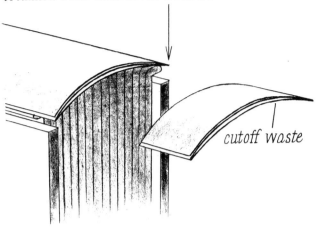

cutoff waste

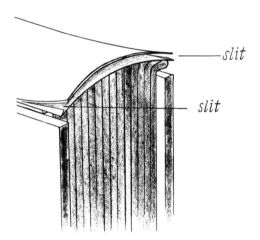

slit

slit

trimming the waste from panel A

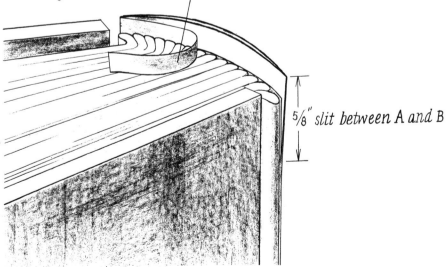

$\frac{5}{8}"$ slit between A and B

199

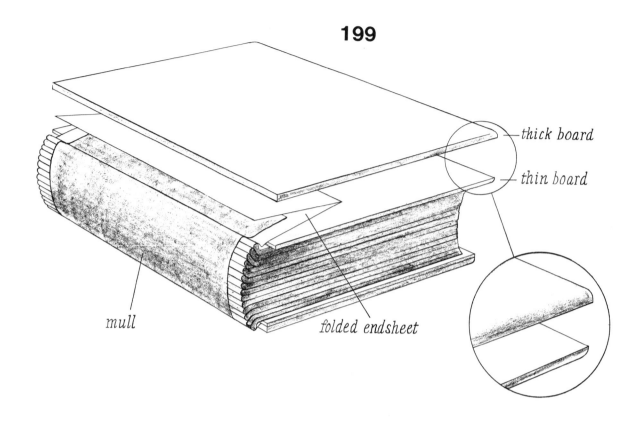

thick board

thin board

mull

folded endsheet

200

201

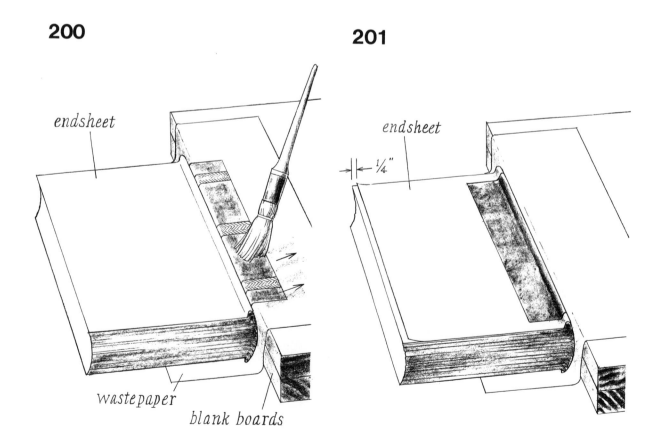

endsheet

wastepaper

blank boards

endsheet

¼"

7
Split
Cover Boards

Split boards are especially appropriate for very large, heavy books whose weight requires maximum support and the strongest possible construction. The boards illustrated here are laminated in two layers, with the tapes and mull sandwiched between (**199**). The lamination in itself greatly stiffens the boards, while the tapes and mull—ordinarily visible under the pasted-down endsheets—are completely concealed.

Cut four boards the same size: a pair of lightweight ones and another pair from heavier caliper board. The thin boards go next to the sewn signatures with the tapes and mull attached to their outside surfaces, while the thicker boards are laminated on top of them. Slightly round the *outside edges only* of all four boards; leave their meeting edges sharp and clean as cut.

First attach one of the thin boards. Lay the mull over onto a blank board on a sheet of wastepaper. Paste the mull, then lay the tapes over on top of it and paste them as well (**200**). Pick up the mull and tapes and fold them back onto the endsheet (**201**). Rub the mull down well using a rubbing sheet. Then trim ¼ inch off the fore edge of the endsheet and slide a clean piece of wastepaper under it. Paste the endsheet and the mull (**202**), discard the soiled

202

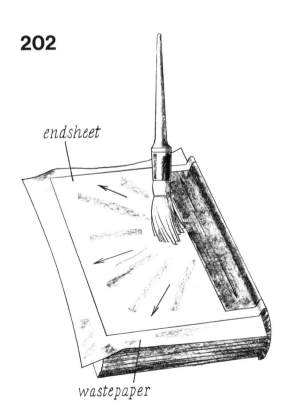

endsheet

wastepaper

203

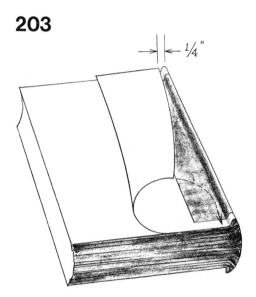

¼"

204

thin cover board

folded flap

check the square

wastepaper

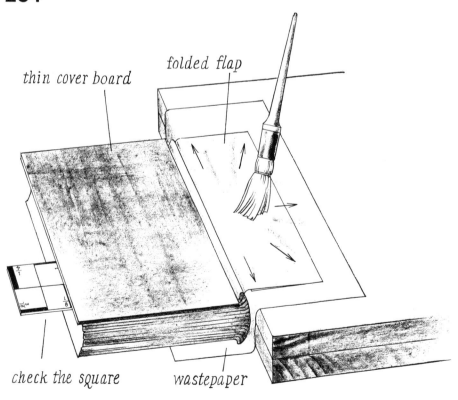

wastepaper, then fold the endsheet back on it-self to a point ¼ inch from the shoulder (**203**). Cover the work with a rubbing sheet and rub it down well.

Turn this folded flap over onto the blank board and paste the inside of the flap. Lay the thin cover board in place on the book, check-ing to see that there is a uniform square around its three sides (**204**). Hold the board firmly to prevent it from slipping while you bring the pasted flap over on top of it (**205**). Cover the work with a rubbing sheet and rub the flap down until dry.

Complete the lamination of this cover by pasting the thick board and attaching it to the thin one, making sure that the edges of both boards are aligned flush all around (**206**). Turn the book over and attach the other boards the same way. Then put the book under heavy weights to dry overnight. Finally, sand-paper the edges of the boards to clean off any squeezed-out paste.

205

206

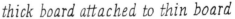
thick board attached to thin board

8

Headbanding

207

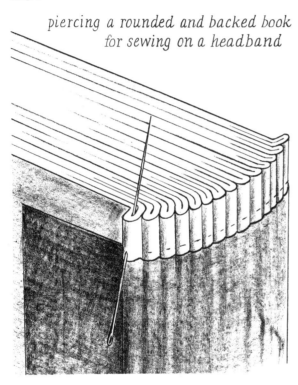

piercing a rounded and backed book for sewing on a headband

208

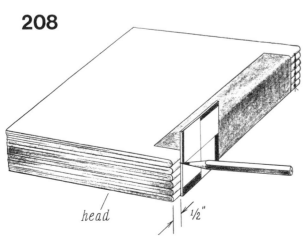

head   ½"

This is a method of reinforcing the head of a book—and not infrequently the foot—by sewing a cord across the tops of the signatures to form a strong cap that not only strengthens the book's construction but also prevents damaging the backbone of the binding when it is pulled from the shelf. A headband distributes this strain equally among all the signatures, and when it is sewn in two contrasting colors, the alternating bands lend an attractive and decorative finish.

In modern machine binding, headbands are cut from a continuously woven strip and simply glued to the backs of the signatures purely as a decoration, without contributing in any way to the strength of the book.

The series of illustrations here show a headband sewn on a square back book. The technique is similar for a rounded and backed book, but because of the shoulders formed by backing, extra care must be taken to see that the piercing and sewing are located as nearly as possible in the centers of the signatures (**207**).

First mark up for piercing holes in the centers of the signatures. Stand the squared card against the back of the book, and draw a pencil line across the signatures about ½ inch down from the head (**208**). If this conflicts with the position of the kettlestitches, shift the line a bit above them.

Secure the book upright in the press between blank boards with about half the book projecting. In this position the signatures can more easily be spread open a bit for more convenient work. Cut a piece of ⅛-inch-thick cardboard measuring 2 × 4 inches, and round one long edge with sandpaper. Slide this *piercing card* inside the center of the first signature, pushed in as far as possible (**209**). Hold it there with one hand. With the other set the piercing awl on the pencil mark and push the awl through the signature and into the edge of the cardboard. Pierce each signature in the same way, putting folded slips of paper in the center of each as you go, to simplify finding them again (**210**).

Cut a piece of cord a trifle smaller in diameter than the square of the book covers and 4 inches longer than the width of the backbone. Use a smooth, tightly woven or braided cord with good body. Smooth cord is better than the sort with "whiskers," which interfere with winding the colored strands. To stiffen the cord for easier manipulation, wax it by drawing it several times across the beeswax cake or pasting it lightly with the fingers.

209

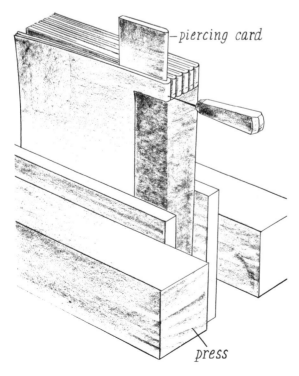

—piercing card

press

210

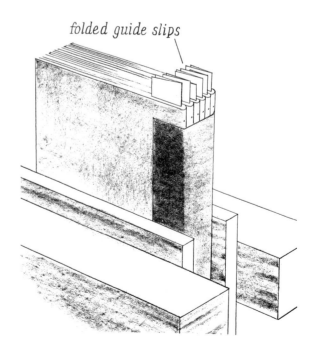

folded guide slips

211

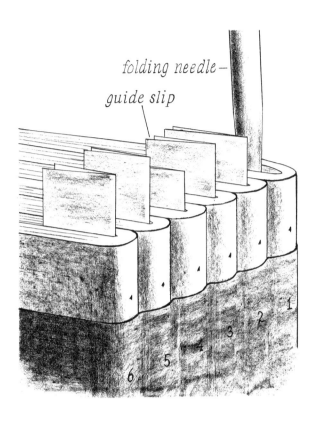

folding needle—

guide slip

Thread a needle with a 16-inch length of white embroidery twist, and a second needle with the same length of green twist. Tie the free ends of both threads together in a knot. For this two-color headband, the white is sewn through the signatures and around the cord, while the green will be wound only around it to fill the spaces between signatures. Where they encircle the cord, both colors should be packed one against the other as tightly as possible to completely conceal the cord, and drawn up snug with a bit of tension.

Start the headband on signature No. 1. Insert the folding needle inside the paper guide slip to locate the center of the signature and spread it open a little (**211**). Pick up the white needle (let the green hang free) and push it through the hole from the outside, angling it up toward the head of the book (**212**). Catch the needle and draw the thread up tight against the knot (**213**). Lay the cord in place across the head of the book. Take the white up over the cord and out again through the same hole

212

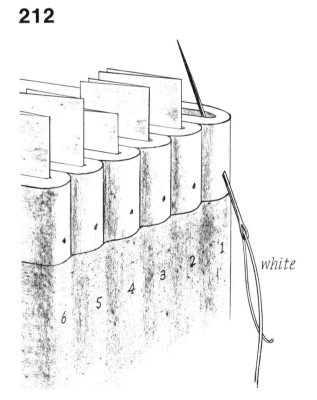

white

213

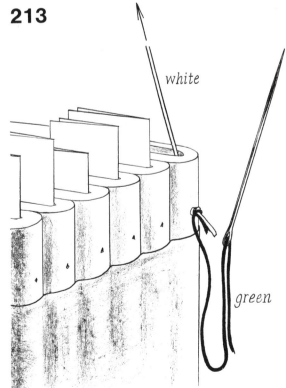

white

green

(**214**), then draw the thread through and pull it snug to hold the cord down firmly on top of the signature (**215**). Now tie the white onto the starting knot to keep this first stitch from working loose. Next wind two loops of white around the cord (**216**). To bind this much of the work together, loop the white thread *under the cord* and around the white strands (**217**), then take it down the back of the signature and tie it onto the starting knot (**218**).

Let the white thread hang free and take up the green. The green loops around the cord fill the gap between the first and second signatures. Wind two loops of green around the cord (**219**) and pack them up tight against the white ones with the fingers. After winding the green, let it hang free at the back for the moment.

214

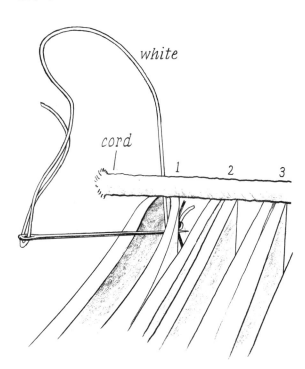

215

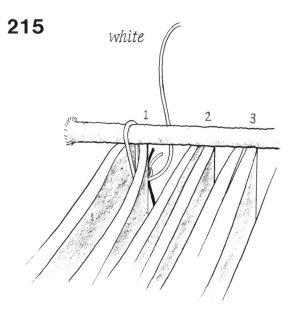

216

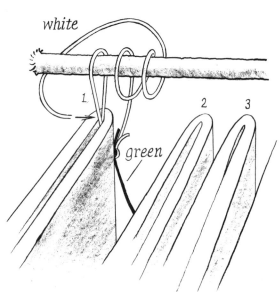

217

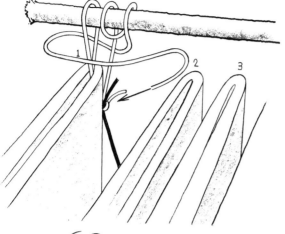

1   *white — down the back*   2   3   4

218

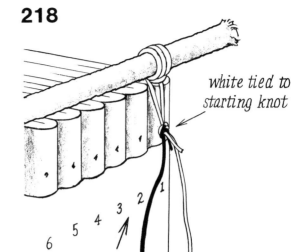

white tied to starting knot

6   5   4   3   2   1

219

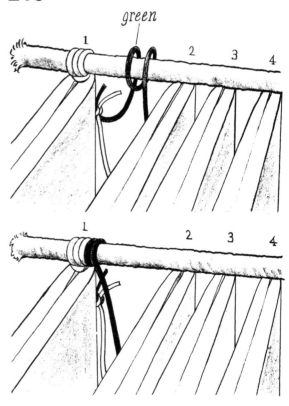

green

220

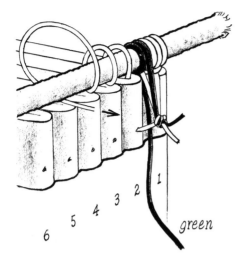

221

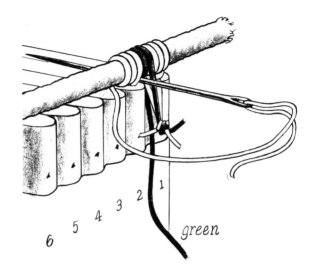

222

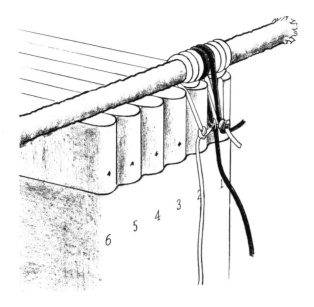

223

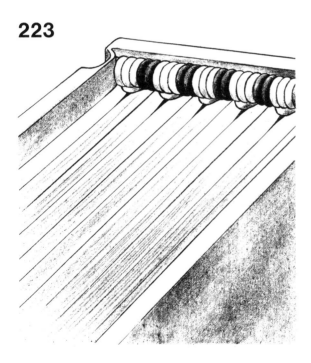

Pick up the white again, take it over across the green strand that is hanging free, and into the hole in the No. 2 signature (**220**). Make three loops of white, then insert the needle between the white and green windings (**221**), loop it around under the cord as before, and draw it up snug. Take the white down the back and tie it to the white thread where it enters this second signature (**222**). Pick up the green again, draw it snug, and tie it to the crossing white strand (**222**). Then wind two loops of green around the cord as before, and continue in this way, working the white and green alternately to the last signature. Tie the last knot and trim both colors, leaving ½-inch tails beyond the knot.

Leave the surplus ends of the cord uncut until it is time to attach the cover boards. Then trim the ends of the cord back to within ³/₃₂ inch of the colored windings. Touch the raw ends of the cord with paste to prevent them from fraying and the windings of embroidery twist from slipping off. The ends of the headband should butt neatly into the hinges of the binding (**223**).

Before beginning on an actual binding, it is useful to make two or three trial headbands using three or four discarded magazines as "signatures." Use only the saddle-stapled kind—not side-stapled. Clamp the magazines in the press with their top and back edges evenly aligned. Use a short piece of clothesline or ⅜-inch wooden dowel for the "cord," and a good big needle and two colors of string in place of embroidery twist. At this greatly enlarged scale everything can be seen clearly, the materials manipulated more easily, and the procedure followed with a minimum of confusion.

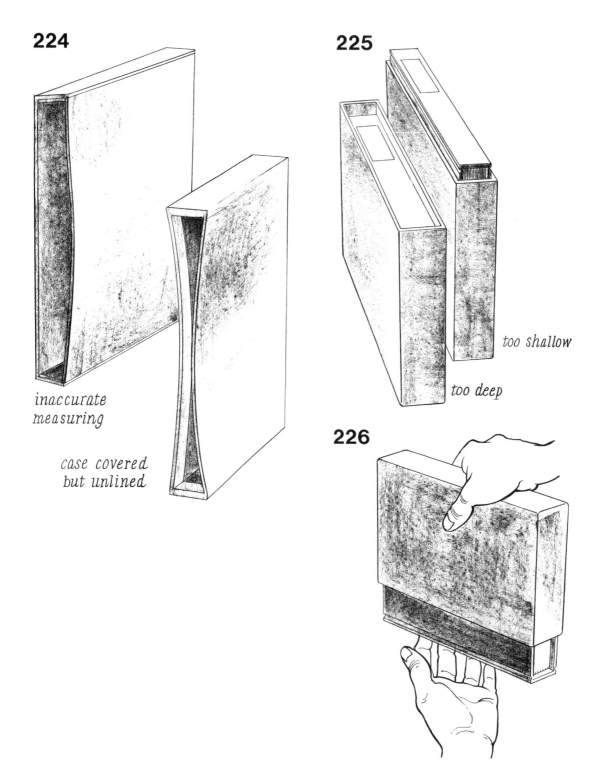

224

*inaccurate
measuring*

*case covered
but unlined*

225

too shallow

too deep

226

9

Making a Slipcase

Order of Work

MEASURE BOOK TO BE CASED

LAY OUT CUTTING DIAGRAM

CUT OUT, LINE INSIDE

SCORE AND FOLD

ASSEMBLE

COVER OUTSIDE OF CASE

PRESS

227

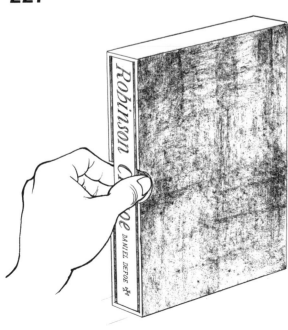

A slipcase is an open-edged box tailored to the book's exact dimensions and intended to protect it from dust, rough handling, and fluctuations in atmospheric conditions. When it is made immediately upon completion of the binding itself, a slipcase also provides a mild clamping action to hold the freshly pasted work until thorough drying has taken place.

The case described here is simple in construction yet strong and durable. Nothing, however, is more important than accurate measuring and a good fit (**224, 225**). A properly made case permits the book to slip out when it is upended (**226**). If the slipcase is made with too loose a fit, the book will drop out and may be damaged, while if the case is too tight, just as much damage will be caused by pulling the book out. Although finger holes are sometimes cut in the sides of the case to remedy this fault (**227**), more often than not they merely concentrate all the strain—and all

228

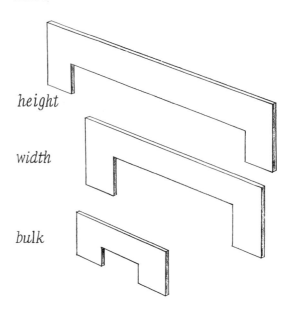

height

width

bulk

229

height   *width*   *bulk*

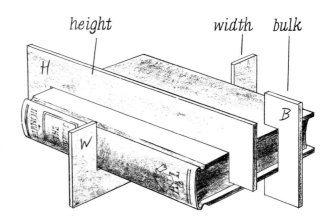

the damage—in one place on the backbone of the book.

This is a one-piece slipcase made from a sheet of lightweight illustration board. Measure the height, width, and bulk (thickness) of the book. From these preliminary measurements make three cardboard jigs, deliberately making them scant of the actual dimensions (**228**). Then carefully pare, trim, and fit each jig to the book at its widest points until they will slip easily over the book (**229**). They should be a loose push-fit to allow room for the extra thicknesses of paper and cloth with which the case will be lined and covered. If you inadvertently trim off too much of an edge, discard the jig and make a new one.

Using the jigs as measuring sticks, lay out a cutting and folding diagram on the illustration board as shown in the diagram (**230**). The dimensions in the diagram are based on 1/16-inch-thick illustration board. Use the car-

230

slipcase: cutting and folding diagram

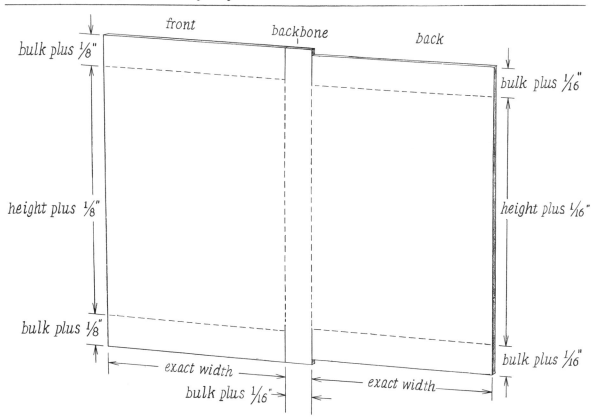

front   backbone   back

bulk plus 1/8"

bulk plus 1/16"

height plus 1/8"

height plus 1/16"

bulk plus 1/8"

bulk plus 1/16"

exact width

bulk plus 1/16"

exact width

penter's square and a sharp pencil for the layout, otherwise the case will not fold up accurately. This case is made as one box with the back folded inside the front (**231**).

Use a sharp knife and the square to cut out the case, cutting only on the solid lines of the diagram (**230**). The dotted lines indicate the edges to be scored and folded. Do not fold up the case at this point. The lining is attached while the case is flat.

Select lining paper and cut a single sheet to fit the inside of the case, as shown in the illustration (**232**). Paste the wrong side of the lining and lay it down on the flat case, adjusting its position so that the edges of the case and the lining are in good alignment. Lay a rubbing sheet over the work and rub it down well, working from the center toward the edges. Then replace the rubbing sheet with waxed paper and a piece of cardboard, and put the work under heavy weights to dry overnight. Complete drying is essential, because attempt-

231

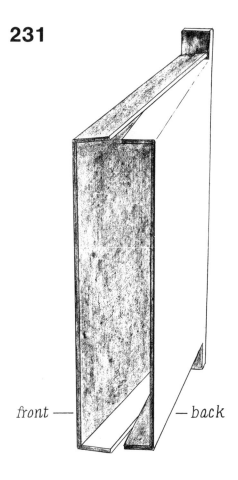

front —   — back

232

slipcase: lining diagram

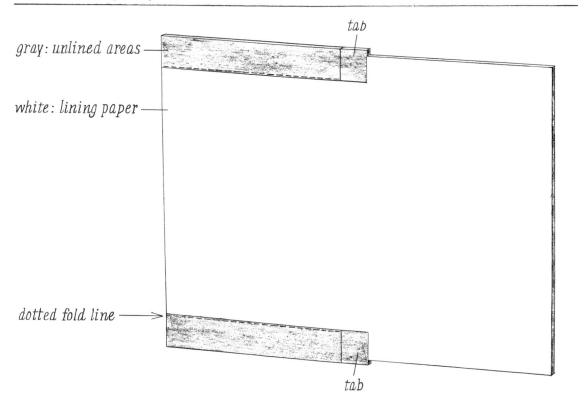

gray: unlined areas —

white: lining paper —

tab

dotted fold line —→

tab

233

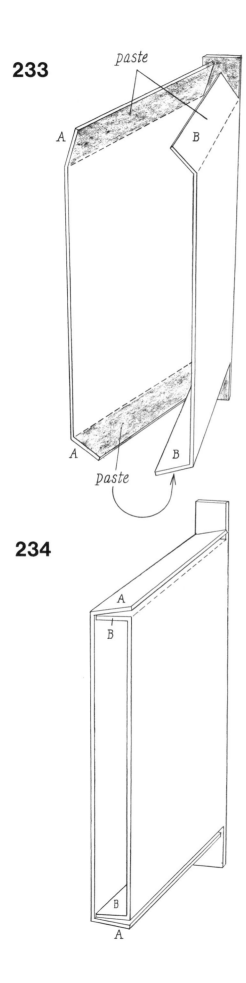

paste

A

B

A

B

paste

234

A

B

B

A

ing to score and fold the case while it is damp will buckle and tear the lining paper.

When the case is dry, lay it inside up flat on the bench. Use the steel ruler and the measuring jigs as needed to redraw the fold lines with light pencil marks. Align the carpenter's square with the marks, and score the fold lines with the folding needle, using good firm pressure. Fold up the case. Scoring and folding techniques are described in detail in the section on making a dust jacket, pages 68–71.

Assemble the slipcase. This work is best done over a wooden last held in the press. An adequate last can be made from a piece of white pine ¾ inch thick, 5 inches wide, and 12 inches long. Plane the ends square, and sandpaper all the surfaces smooth. Tape layers of cardboard to one side of the last as needed to build up its thickness to equal the book's bulk.

Clamp the last on end in the press. Brush a thin coat of paste on the A and B flaps of the slipcase (**233**). Do not paste the tabs. Close up the case with the B flaps inside the A flaps (**234**), and slide the case down over the last (**235**). Rub the pasted flaps down well with a

235

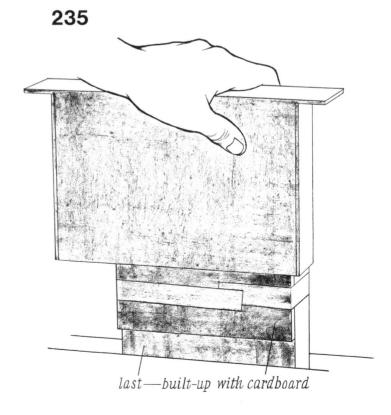

last—built-up with cardboard

236

tab

tab

237

9/16"

9/16"

238 *slit fore edge*

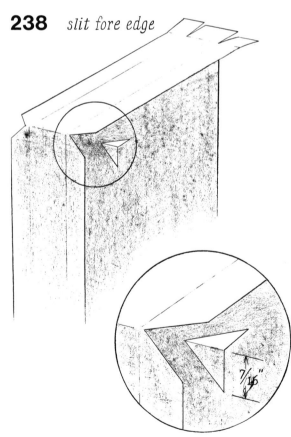

7/16"

239

folding needle

240

paper side panel

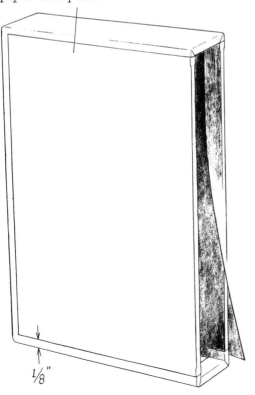

$\frac{1}{8}''$

clean cloth while holding the case firmly on the last. Continue rubbing until the flaps are well stuck together.

When the case is dry, trim the two tabs flush with the case and slightly round their edges and back corners with extrafine sandpaper held over a block (**236**).

Cover the outside of the case. The edges—top, bottom, and backbone—are covered with cloth and the sides with paper panels. Cut a piece of cloth 1 inch wider than the width of the backbone and 1⅛ inches longer than the distance around the edges from one open side to the other (**237**). Paste the cloth, let it stand a minute or two, then paste it again. Lay the cloth on the top edge of the case, extending 9/16 inch beyond its open front edge. Check to see that there is an equal overhang on the sides. Smooth the cloth down and rub it gently with a clean cloth. Then draw it down the backbone and around onto the bottom edge, checking the overhangs as you go. Put the case on the last and rub the cloth down, especially well over the box's edges. Snip out the back corners top and bottom to make 45-degree miters, and slit the fore edges top and bottom (**238**).

Paste the turnovers either side of the backbone and turn these in first. Then paste down the head and foot turnovers. Blunt the sharp back corners by tapping them with the side of the flat folder. Finally, paste and turn in the head and foot tabs, ironing them flat and creasing them sharply into the corners with the folding needle (**239**).

Make the paper side panels, allowing a ⅛-inch margin around three sides of the case and ½-inch turnovers at the open front edges (**240**). Paste the panels and attach them, checking the margins all around. Put the case on the last and rub the panels down until dry. Then paste and turn in the fore edges, using the folding needle to crease in the inside corners.

Tape the book in waxed paper and slide it into the case. Cover both sides of the case with waxed paper and lay the work flat under weights to dry overnight.

241

box : cutting and folding diagram

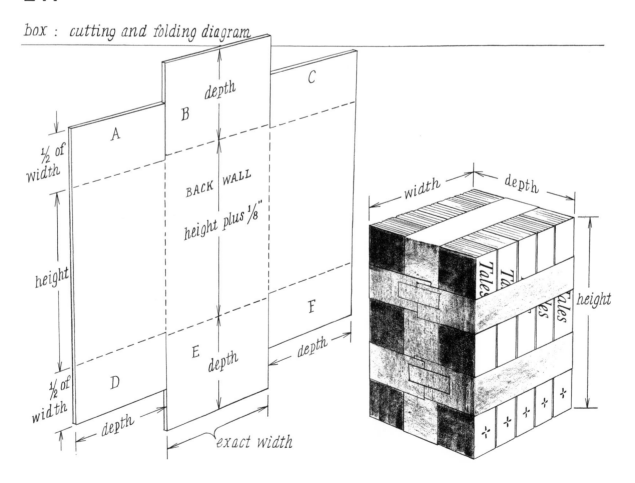

A

½ of width

B

depth

C

BACK WALL

height plus ⅛"

height

E

depth

F

D

½ of width

depth

depth

exact width

width

depth

height

Tales

10

Boxing a Set of Books

Order of Work

STRAP AND MEASURE BOOKS

LAY OUT CUTTING DIAGRAM

CUT OUT BOX

LINE INSIDE OF BACK

SCORE AND FOLD

COVER OUTSIDE

LINE INSIDE

This is a one-piece box similar in construction to the slipcase. The number, size, and weight of the books in the set should govern the weight of board from which the box is to be made. The box is designed with a double layer of board at the top and bottom for strength. The lining is attached in two stages: the back wall with the box flat and unfolded, and the remaining interior surfaces after the box has been assembled.

Strap the set of books together with bands of taped kraft paper. Then make three jigs as described in the section on Making a Slipcase, page 127. Transfer the dimensions to a cutting and folding diagram laid out on a single sheet of board, using the jigs and the carpenter's square (**241**). This diagram is based on 1/16-inch-thick illustration board. Cut out the box, cutting only along the solid lines of the diagram. The dotted lines indicate edges that are

242

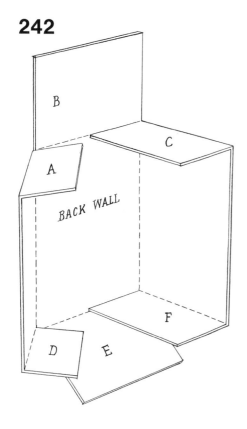

BACK WALL

243

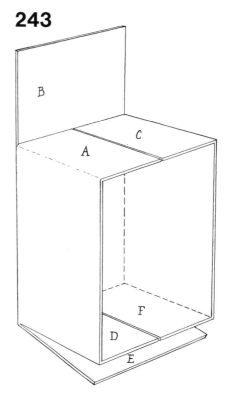

244

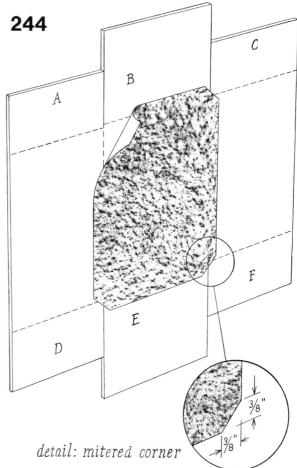

detail: mitered corner

245

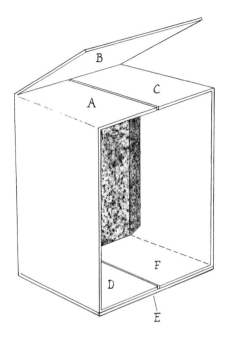

246

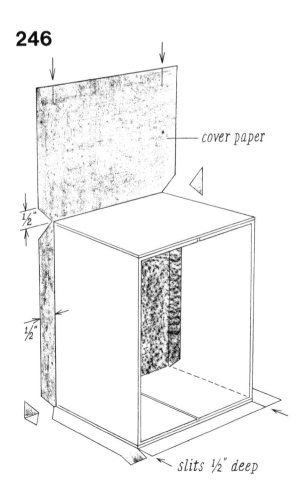

cover paper

½"

½"

slits ½" deep

to be scored and folded after the back wall has been lined. The box is folded and assembled as shown in illustrations (**242**) and (**243**). Do not fold up the box at this point. The lining is attached while the box is flat.

Cut and attach the back wall lining (**244**). Note that this lining laps over the inside back corners of the box on all four sides, and that these corners are mitered 45 degrees. Rub the lining down well, especially around the edges, then put the work flat under a blank board and heavy weights until it is thoroughly dry.

When this much of the work is completely dry, score (on the inside of the box) for the folds, shown as dotted lines in the cutting and folding diagram (**241**).

Assemble the box. Before pasting, it is well to fold up the box on the scored lines to check the work for a good fit. Fold all the scored lines, close up the box as shown in (**243**), and secure it with a wide band of kraft paper taped tightly around the sides. Slide the strapped set of books inside. If all is well, remove the books and open the box out flat again.

Start the final assembly with the bottom. Paste the outside of flaps D and F and the inside of flap E. As a wooden last is impractical here, the simplest procedure is to fold the pasted flaps together, then stand the box on the bench and rub the flaps down dry from the inside (**245**). Lay a wooden board inside the box and place heavy weights on it, leaving the work to dry for an hour. Paste up the corresponding flaps of the top of the box and assemble it in the same way. Tape the strapped set of books in waxed paper and slide it into the box. Lay a piece of cardboard on top and set the work aside under weights to dry thoroughly. Then lightly sand the outside edges of the box to make a smooth foundation for attaching the covering paper. Remove the books.

Cover the outside of the box. Cut a single sheet of paper to cover the top, back, and bottom, allowing ½-inch turnovers as shown in the illustration (**246**). Paste and attach the paper, checking the turnovers all around. Then snip out the four back corners to make 45-degree miters, and slit the fore edges top and bottom (**246**). Paste and attach the turnovers, starting with the back. Then turn in the top and bottom, and finally the fore edges. Iron down and crease the inside corners with the folding needle (**247**).

Cut paper panels to cover the sides of the box. Allow a ⅛-inch margin on three sides and ½-inch turnovers at the fore edges (**248**). One at a time, paste and attach the side panels, rubbing them down well, especially around the edges where they lap over the cloth. Paste and attach the fore edge turnovers, creasing the inside corners with the folding needle.

Complete the lining with a single band of paper long enough to cover all four walls of the

247

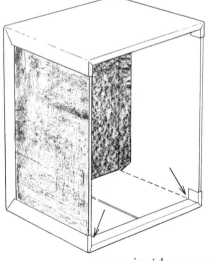

crease inside corners

248

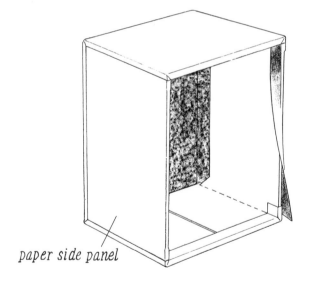

paper side panel

box with an additional ½-inch lap at the upper left-hand corner (**249**). Allow for a ⅛-inch margin around the fore edges. (**250**). To attach the lining, fold and crease the ½-inch lap. Lay the box on its side. As promptly as possible, paste the lining and attach the lap end first. Smooth the paper along the side, over the bottom and around to the starting corner again, creasing the paper well into the corners with the fingers and the folding stick. Keep the fore edge margins to a uniform ⅛ inch. With a clean cloth, rub all the surfaces down well, making sure that the edges of the paper are well stuck, particularly where they lap over the cloth and paper turnovers of the outer covering.

Promptly slide the strapped set of books into the box. Lay the box on its side, cover it with clean waxed paper, and set it aside under weights to dry overnight.

249

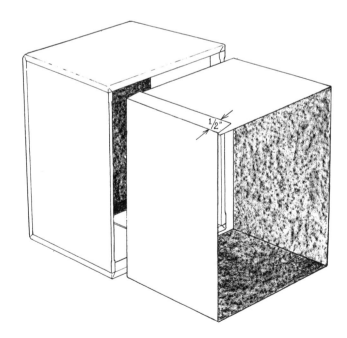

250

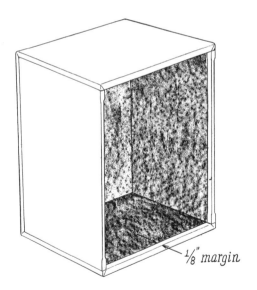

11

Designing Labels

251

Order of Work

MAKE ROUGH TRIALS

MAKE FINISHED LAYOUT

EXECUTE FINAL LETTERING

LET DRY

CLEAN OFF PENCIL LINES

APPLY SEALER

CUT OUT AND ATTACH LABEL

PRESS

Titling is a necessary detail of bookbinding and should be planned in conjunction with the selection and color of cover material, headband twist, and cover paper and cloth for slipcases and boxes. Whether a dust jacket, folio, manuscript, or music, the contents should be identified with the essential information.

Books covered with cloth or paper can be fitted with paper labels pasted to the backbone or front cover, as was once quite customary. Labels are relatively simple to produce if you have a printing press, but hand-lettered ones are just as professional when designed and executed with care.

The label should be legible and in harmony with the character, size, and general appearance of the binding. The sizes of the title elements are usually ranked in descending order by title, author, and publisher, although this is not a hard-and-fast rule. More often it is the available space—for example the width of the backbone—that chiefly determines the size and extent of the lettering. Keep in mind also that capital letters take up more space than lowercase, while italics and cursive lettering are more compact.

In the case of long titles and authors' names, it is accepted practice to make abbreviations and omissions, using only the author's last name and a shortened title, eliminating subtitles altogether (**251**). For example, *Printing Types: their History, Forms, and Use,* by Daniel Berkeley Updike, can be condensed to read simply *Printing Types,* Updike. The shorter word *Types* might conceivably occupy the full width of the label with *Printing* done in smaller italics. Contrast can also be introduced by lettering *Types* not in black but in a color that harmonizes with those of the binding itself. In the case of music, the essential information would include the composer's last name, the title of the work, and possibly the opus number.

It is important to make a few experimental label sketches to work out the general design, the relative sizes of the lettering, and the spacing and color. These can be made in pencil on cheap paper, cut to size and laid on the binding for study (**252**). Try different shapes and sizes with the lettering sketched in black and colored pencil. In a case where the lettering is to be done directly on the binding, trials can be made in ink or chinese white on clear acetate. A slender volume of poetry may require only the simplest rectangular label on the front cover. In fact, its backbone may be so thin that any other solution is out of the question. For a bulkier book of larger dimensions, the author and title can be run up the full height of the backbone. In designing any label, remember that hand-lettered titles invariably take up more space than printed ones and that the smaller the lettering, the more exacting it is to execute.

The same principles apply to printed

252

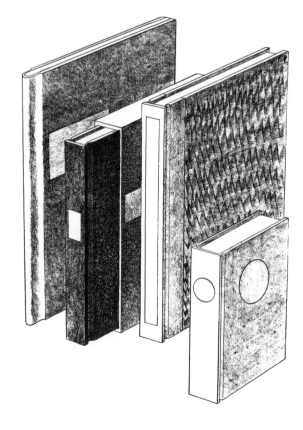

labels. The typeface and point size should be chosen with the character of the book and binding in mind. The letterspacing should be worked out on rough pencil sketches before setting the type. Careful makeready is of course important. When you are ready to print the finished job, make a dozen proofs and then select the one that is the most uniformly black and crisp. And, of course, allow the ink to dry thoroughly before attaching the label to the binding.

When these preliminaries have been completed, make a finished pencil layout on good quality paper. Single-ply pen-and-ink paper is ideal for even the finest pen lettering and has good opacity. Avoid rough or soft papers, as the fibers clog the pen point and spread the ink or color, making it nearly impossible to get the crispness that distinguishes good lettering. Heavy, stiff paper is generally out of scale for most books and is particularly tedious and difficult to paste down successfully.

Execute the final lettering on a piece of paper generously larger than the label (**253**).

253

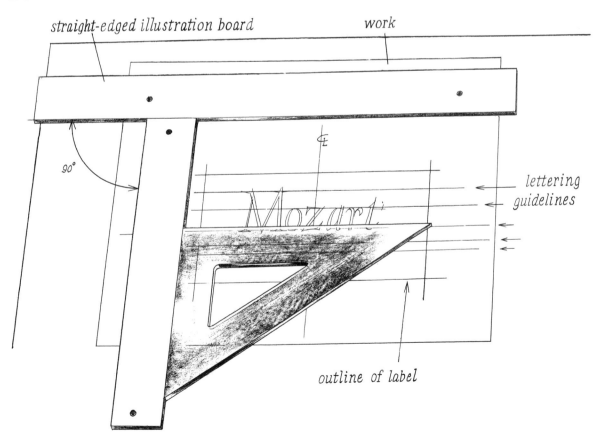

straight-edged illustration board

work

90°

lettering guidelines

outline of label

Tack straight-edged strips of illustration board over the work on a drawing board with the corner an exact 90-degree right angle. Use a triangle to lay out the outline of the label, a vertical center line, and horizontal guidelines for the height of the lettering—both lowercase and capitals—carrying all these horizontal lines out well beyond the label area.

Jet black waterproof india ink is one of the most permanent lettering fluids and works exceptionally well with either pen or brush. If you plan to use a second or third color, water soluble designer's gouache colors and permanent white are ideal for brush lettering. They have high opacity, brush on smoothly, and, when sealed with a thin coat of clear picture varnish, are very durable (**254**). Aerosol workable fixatif applied as two lightly sprayed coats is another satisfactory sealer. In either case, the lettering must be thoroughly dry before the sealer is applied—dried for at least twenty-four hours. And because inks, pigments, varnishes, and sealers are chemical compounds, they should be tested in advance on scraps of the same materials you are using.

To avoid smudging the lettering in progress, work with your hands resting on a clean rubbing sheet taped or laid over the area just under the label area. The slight moisture of the skin is enough to blur the lettering, and this should be approached as a one-shot execution with no retouching.

When lettering with a broad-nib pen, use clean, incisive strokes. Avoid going back over them. If you make a mistake, discard the label and begin again. However expertly done, retouching with white can never be made invisible, and it will in all probability turn yellow when varnished.

When the lettering is completed—and proofread to catch any typographical errors—set the work aside, drawing board and all, to dry for at least overnight. Then clean off the pencil guidelines with gentle strokes of a soft eraser, naturally making sure to leave the lines that outline the label itself. While the work is

254

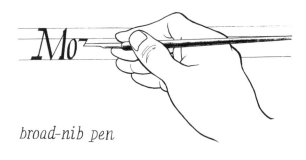

broad-nib pen

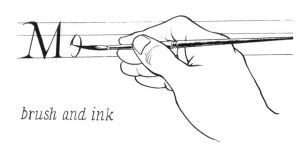

brush and ink

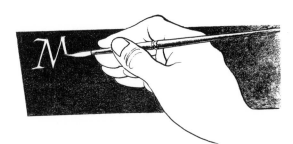

permanent white on colored paper

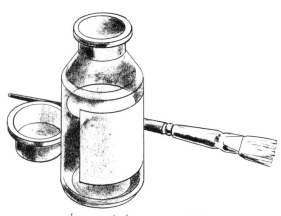

clear picture varnish

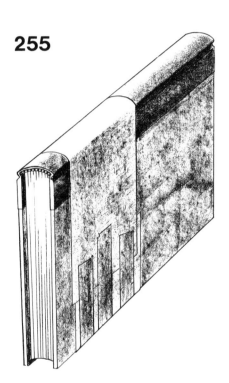

255

still tacked down flat, apply a very thin coat of varnish or fixatif over the entire label and well past its edges. Allow the label to dry untouched overnight.

To cut out the label, remove the tacks or pins and lay the whole sheet of paper on a smooth piece of cardboard. Use a sharp X-Acto knife and the steel ruler aligned with the pencil outlines. Hold the ruler down firmly and use enough pressure on the knife to cut the paper completely on the first stroke.

Attach the label. Lay it on a clean sheet of wastepaper, and use a small brush to spread a thin coat of paste, working from the center of the label toward the edges. Hold the label securely to prevent its slipping, so that no paste is transferred to its face. To paste the corners where your fingers have been holding the label steady, pick up the label on the end of the brush and transfer it paste-side up to clean wastepaper. Lay the label down, then hold it there with a fingernail while you touch paste on those two last corners. Pick up the label with the brush again and lay it in position on the binding. Cover it with waxed paper. Hold the waxed paper from slipping and rub the label down gently but thoroughly. Discard the waxed paper. Replace it with a clean sheet and put the work under weights to dry thoroughly. If the label is to be attached to the backbone, clamp it down firmly with a band of paper drawn tight around the book and fastened with tape (**255**).

12

Making Tools and Equipment

The tools and pieces of equipment included here can be manufactured inexpensively with ordinary woodworking tools from readily available woods, metals, and fasteners, in many cases from leftovers and scrap materials.

Use dry hardwoods such as maple, birch, beech, walnut, or cherry, all of which will take a high finish. Sharpen the woodworking tools and hone their cutting edges as necessary while the work progresses. Lay out and check the work with a square, and use the miter box whenever possible to ensure clean, smooth saw cuts.

Make all cuts a fraction wide of the mark, then dress the edge to size with a sharp plane or a double-cut file and 220- and 320-grit sandpaper. Because these binding tools will be used on paper, cloth, and other fragile materials, their surfaces must be as smooth as possible and maintained clean and dry to prevent scarring or staining the work.

When the wooden pieces have been cut to size, shaped, and finish-sanded, apply a thinned first coat of polyurethane. Allow this coat to stand until hard dry. Then fine-sand it, wipe it clean with a tack rag, and apply one or two additional full-strength coats of urethane rubbed down between coats with 600-grit wet-or-dry silicon carbide paper and mineral oil. This treatment is preferable to using steel wool, particles of which tend to become imbedded in the urethane. Wipe the finished work with a clean damp cloth, then allow it to dry. Do not use oil finishes, as there is usually enough residue to stain paper even after several weeks' drying.

When joining wooden parts, use a combination of screws and a good waterproof glue, leaving the work in clamps to dry overnight. Metal fasteners such as bolts, washers, and nuts should be scrubbed with a toothbrush and paint thinner to remove the coating of factory machine oil, and the nuts run back and forth several times on the bolts to make sure there are no burrs to obstruct their free operation.

Awl (256)

This handmade awl is superior to commercial ones, which usually have much too thick a shank and consequently pierce holes too large in diameter for the best sewing.

Cut a piece of dry white pine to the dimensions shown in the illustration, then use a block plane, a double-cut file, and sandpaper to give the handle a comfortable shape. Stand the handle on end and make a pilot hole for the needle by driving a ¾-inch No. 20 wire nail straight into the handle not quite to the head. Remove the nail.

Break off the eye of a 2-inch sharps needle by holding it with a pair of pliers while snapping off the eye with another. Insert the broken end of the needle in the pilot hole. Put the needle in a metal vise or hold it tight in a large pair of pliers with about ½ inch of the broken end projecting. Pick up the awl handle, start it over the needle, then push it on firmly up against the pliers. Leave about 1⅛ inches of the needle exposed. Sand the handle with 320-grit sandpaper and apply the finish.

256

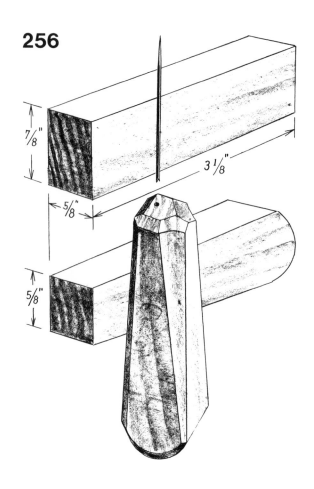

257

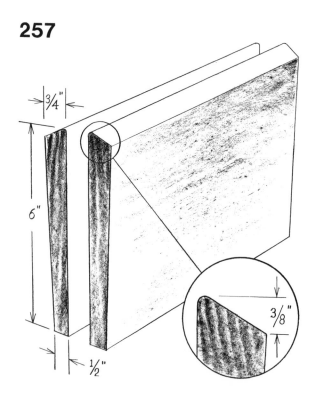

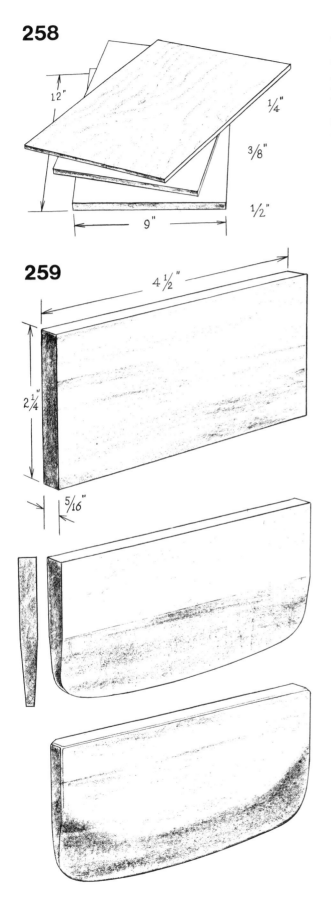

258

259

Backing boards (257)

These boards should be made of close-grained hardwood lumber that is flat—not warped, bowed, or twisted. Maple is ideal. It is strong, stiff, and has high resistance to denting and bruising. As they are meant to drop well down into the press, they should be made ½ inch shorter than the distance between the press screws. Plane and sand their inside surfaces as smooth as possible. Taper their outside surfaces as shown to prevent their being driven down into the press and out of alignment while backing a book. Plane the ⅜-inch top bevels as nearly alike as you can, then use 120-grit sandpaper to carefully round their extreme top edges to the shape of a book's shoulder. Sand the bevels, then apply the finish. Give the end-grain edges at least two coats to minimize warping.

Blank boards (258)

Three or four boards of various thicknesses are almost indispensable for supporting the work in the several stages of binding, as well as for pressing. Before applying the finish, sand their surfaces and edges as smooth as possible and slightly round their sharp edges with fine sandpaper held over a wooden block.

Flat folder (259)

Cut a piece of hardwood to the dimensions shown in the illustration. Use a coping saw and block plane to round the corners and trim the bottom edge to a uniform contour. Then with the plane taper the sides from the middle toward the bottom edge. With 80-grit sandpaper and a double-cut file, taper these same sections toward the ends, letting the tapers follow the curvature of the bottom edge. These are the working parts of the folder, and their edges and surfaces should be made as fair and smooth as possible—with no ridges. Sand thoroughly with 220- and 320-grit paper before applying the finish.

Folding needle (260)

Use a 4¾-inch steel knitting needle with a ⅛-inch diameter. Cut the wooden handle blank to size and draw diagonals on both ends to locate their centers. Drill a test hole in a scrap of wood to find the drill size that will make the needle a tight push-fit. Then drill a hole clear through the handle blank, working from both ends to the center if necessary. Next shape the handle as you wish, tapering the sides and edges to make it comfortable in the hand. Note that the under side of the handle is planed flat—and closer to the needle—to accommodate working in tight places. Sand the handle to final smoothness before applying the finish. Finally, force the handle onto the needle, centered on its length. If the fit is a bit too easy, remove the needle, touch a few drops of glue into the hole with a bamboo skewer, then replace the needle. Wipe the exposed ends of the needle clean of glue with a damp cloth and let the work dry for a few hours.

260

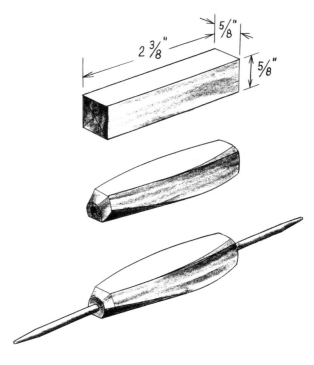

261

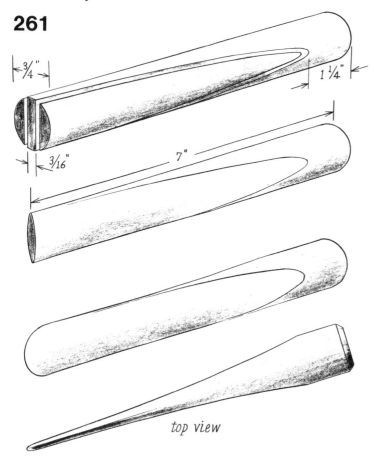

top view

Folding stick (261)

Make two saw cuts from the end of a 7-inch length of ¾-inch hardwood dowel to remove tapered slabs. Use a double-cut file and 80-grit sandpaper wrapped over a flat stick to make both sides slightly convex in the narrow dimension and concave in the length, and to round the end. Sand the edges to a thin but rounded contour as shown in the top view of the illustration. Then sand all the surfaces with 320-grit paper before applying the finish.

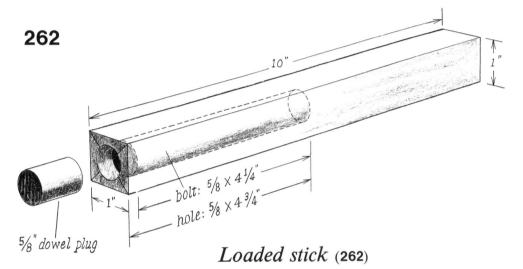

262

10"

1"

1"

bolt: ⅝ × 4¼"

hole: ⅝ × 4¾"

⅝" dowel plug

Loaded stick (262)

This is a simple wooden bar with a section of iron bolt fitted into the working end to give it weight. Cut and plane a length of hardwood to the size given in the illustration. Draw diagonals on one end to locate the center.

Drill a ⅝-inch hole into this end to a depth of 4¾ inches. If a drill press is not available, use a ⅝-inch auger bit and a bit brace. Have someone sight the bit as straight as possible while you bore the hole. Knock out the shavings. Cut off a ⅝-inch bolt with a hacksaw to a length of 4¼ inches after first cutting off the head. File around the sawn ends to remove the sharp burred edges.

Plane the sides of the stick smooth, then sand them well with 320-grit paper held over a wooden block. Slightly round the long edges. Slide the bolt into the hole. It should be an easy push-fit, but if not, file around and around the bolt with a flat mill bastard file. Don't file too much, however, for the bolt must not rattle in the hole.

Push the bolt into the stick. Then glue a 1-inch length of ⅝-inch hardwood dowel and tap it into the hole tight against the end of the bolt. Let the work stand overnight to dry. Trim the end of the stick square, taking off the excess dowel along with about ⅛ inch of the stick. Before applying the finish, round off all the edges and corners of this working end with fine sandpaper.

Mitering jig (263)

Use a dense, stiff material about 1/64-inch thick, such as is used for the covers of manuscript binders available in a mottled brown and other colors. Use the steel ruler, a square, and a sharp knife to cut the jig to size. Then lay out the horizontal and vertical register lines and rule them in black waterproof india ink. Be sure that the intersection of these lines is an exact 90-degree right angle. Next, lay out and

263

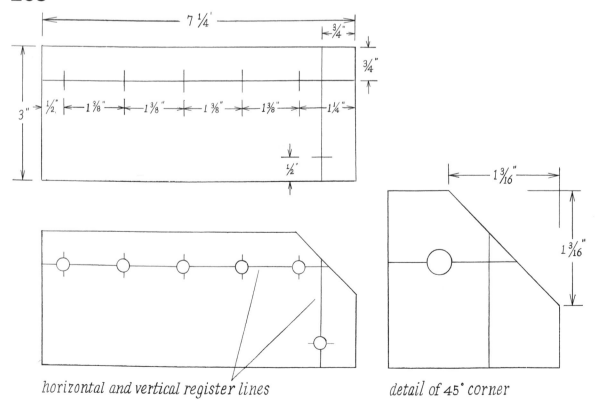

horizontal and vertical register lines   detail of 45° corner

264

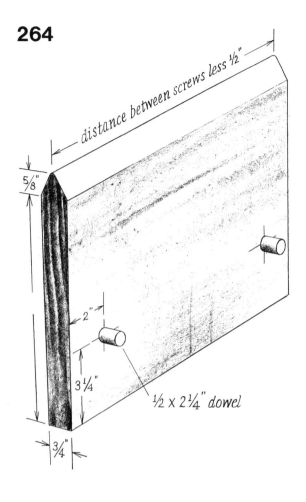

distance between screws less ½"

5/8"

2"

3¼"

½ x 2¼" dowel

¾"

cut the 45-degree angle, using the dimensions in the full-scale detail of the illustration. This jig will work for cover boards up to ⅛ inch in thickness. For heavier boards the position of the 45-degree angle must be shifted out from the corner accordingly. Lay off five marks spaced along the horizontal register line, and one mark on the vertical line. Center a paper punch over each mark and punch a hole. Then coat the entire jig with urethane or spray it with two coats of workable fixatif.

Piercing board (264)

This board is best made from a piece of 1 × 12-inch white pine, with the grain running in the long dimension. As the board is meant to drop down into the press and rest on the dowel stops, its length should be ½ inch less than the distance between the press screws.

Plane bevels on the long top edge to the dimensions given in the illustration. Round the extreme top edge slightly to fit the inside fold of a signature. Then sand all the surfaces to final smoothness—especially the bevels—and apply the finish before gluing in the dowel stops.

After repeated piercing, the beveled top edge of the board will need to be renewed. This is easily done by planing new bevels and refinishing them.

265

lying press, 14" between screws

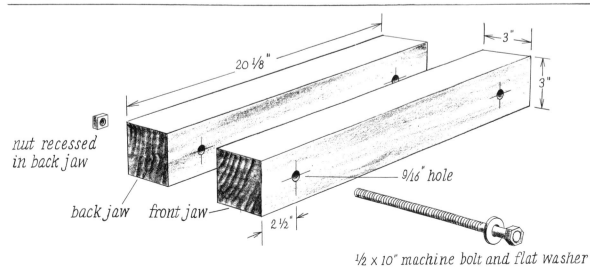

20 ⅛"

3"

3"

nut recessed in back jaw

back jaw   front jaw

9/16" hole

2½"

½ x 10" machine bolt and flat washer

Press and tub (265–269)

This press and its tub, or stand, are strong and will do entirely satisfactory work. The press should be made of good dry hardwood to withstand heavy work, but pine can be used for the tub.

Position and bore the bolt holes in the press as accurately as possible. If a drill press is not available, make a jig by boring a $\frac{9}{16}$-inch hole in a short length of 2-inch stock, while someone sights the auger bit for you. Then clamp the jig to the press jaws in the correct position to guide the auger bit.

Sand the top and meeting surfaces of the press jaws as smooth as possible with 400-grit sandpaper. Then apply two coats of polyurethane, wet-sanded between coats with 600-grit silicon carbide paper. Thoroughly clean the bolts, nuts, and washers with paint thinner to remove all factory oil. Run the nuts back and forth several times on the bolts to make sure nothing obstructs their free movement.

266   *detail: outside of back jaw*

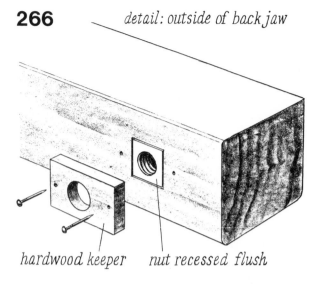

hardwood keeper   *nut recessed flush*

267

tommy bar welded to head of bolt

268

press tub

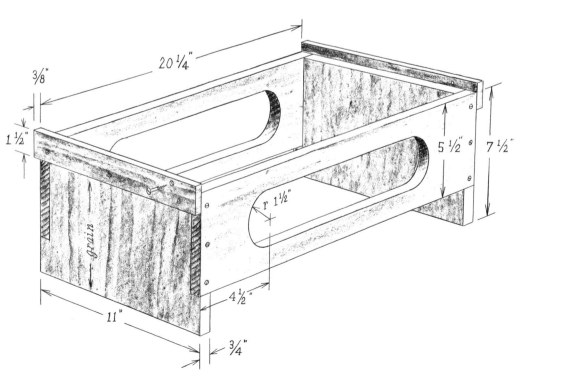

Although the press screws can be operated with a wrench, welding $\frac{1}{4} \times 6$-inch tommy bars to the bolt heads greatly improves the convenience of the press.

Assemble the tub with glue and flathead steel or brass screws. Clamp the joining parts in

269

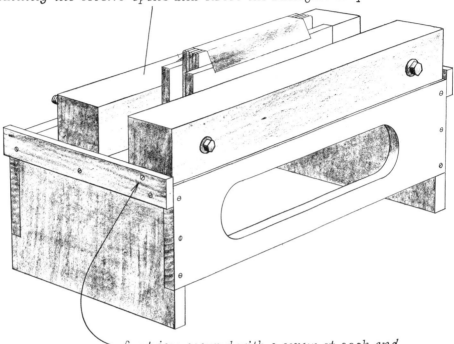

turning the screws opens and closes the back jaw only

front jaw secured with a screw at each end

270

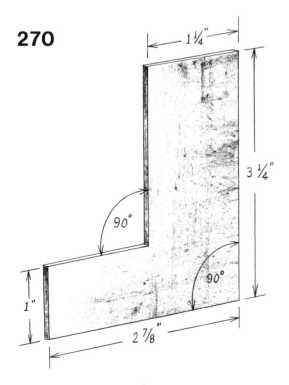

position and drill and countersink pilot holes for the screws. Then take the work apart, glue the joints, and reassemble with screws and clamps. Leave the work in clamps to dry overnight.

Right-angle card (270)

This is in effect a miniature square, particularly useful for squaring up the head of a book just before attaching the mull. Its small size makes it much more convenient to use than a conventional carpenter's try square.

Lay out the work on a piece of good quality 2-ply illustration board, using the square to ensure that both right angles are accurate. Then cut it to shape—again using the square—and finish it with a coat of urethane.

sewing frame

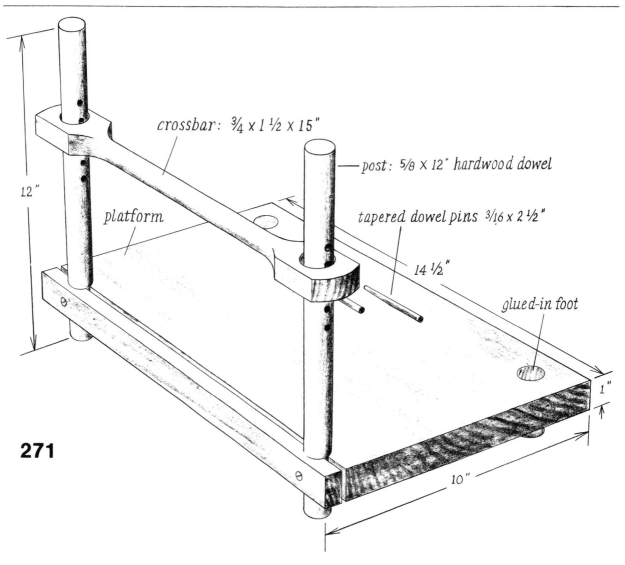

crossbar: ¾ x 1 ½ x 15"

post: ⅝ x 12" hardwood dowel

tapered dowel pins ³⁄₁₆ x 2 ½"

12"

platform

14 ½"

glued-in foot

1"

271

10"

slotted hardwood or plywood key

1 ³⁄₈" 1 ⅝"

¼"

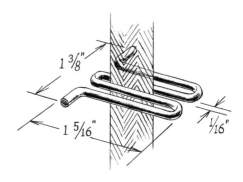

key made from 6-inch length of heavy wire

1 ³⁄₈"

1 ⁵⁄₁₆"

1⁄₁₆"

272

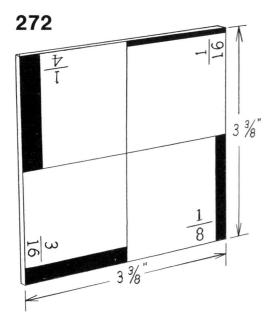

273

¾ x 8 x 10"

¾ x 7 x 9"

½ x 5 x 8"

⅜ x 5 x 7"

Sewing frame (271)

This frame will accommodate all but very large books and works quite as well as a commercial model. Maple is the ideal wood for the platform because its weight helps hold it from sliding during sewing. But satisfactory frames have also been made entirely of white pine. Select a piece of lumber for the platform that is flat—not warped, bowed, or twisted end to end. Plane and sand the top surface smooth, then immediately apply finish to both sides to minimize warping.

The sewing tapes are secured under the platform slot by keys made of maple, plywood, or heavy-gauge wire.

Squared card (272)

Use a piece of good quality 2-ply illustration board, white on both sides. Lay out the dimensions of the card so that all four corners are exact 90-degree right angles. Rule the intersecting center lines with black waterproof india ink. Then rule bands of the different widths and label each section with the designated fraction. To make this card the most useful, prepare the reverse side the same way, with the bands of like width back to back.

Cut out the card, using the square and a sharp knife. Check the work by laying the card inside the angle of the carpenter's square. Minor inaccuracies can be corrected by carefully sanding the edges of the card with 120-grit sandpaper held over a wooden block. Recheck the work and then apply a coat of polyurethane to both sides and let dry.

Wooden lasts (273)

These are simple pieces of white pine, milled or planed to thickness and sanded smooth. Slightly round their edges with sandpaper. The versatility of any one of the lasts shown here can be extended by taping it together with layers of cardboard to equal the required thickness.

Index